PATTERNS OF DERIVATIONAL AFFIXATION
IN THE CABRANIEGO DIALECT OF EAST-CENTRAL ASTURIAN

PATTERNS OF DERIVATIONAL AFFIXATION IN THE CABRANIEGO DIALECT OF EAST-CENTRAL ASTURIAN

BY

YAKOV MALKIEL

UNIVERSITY OF CALIFORNIA PRESS
BERKELEY · LOS ANGELES · LONDON
1970

UNIVERSITY OF CALIFORNIA PUBLICATIONS IN LINGUISTICS

Advisory Editors: W. E. Bull, W. L. Chafe, †C. D. Chrétien, M. B. Emeneau, M. R. Haas,
Harry Hoijer, L. D. Newmark, D. L. Olmsted, William Shipley, R. P. Stockwell

Volume 64

Approved for publication June 19, 1969
Issued March 30, 1970
Price $2.50

University of California Press
Berkeley and Los Angeles
California

University of California Press, Ltd.
London, England

PREFATORY NOTE

The importance of Asturo-Leonese dialects for the study of comparative Romance phonology and inflection has been known since the pioneering studies of A. Fuchs (1840) and E. Gessner (1867). The original, richly diversified material which the lexical deposits of these dialects offer invites likewise the attention of the student of Romance affixation. The present monograph attempts to make a start in this direction by concentrating on a single subdialect rather circumstantially described over thirty years ago: the speech of Cabranes in East-Central Asturias.

The confinement to a single section of the dialect area is not the only step I have taken to reduce the number of unknowns and to narrow the margin of doubt. A parallel measure aiming at the same general goal has been the choice of the descriptive rather than the genetic perspective. Having thus bridled my inclination to engage in comparison and reconstruction, I could afford to strike out the more boldly in other directions. This monograph departs from established practice, first, in operating systematically with the interplay of suffixes, suffixoids, and interfixes—as defined in the introductory sections; and, second, in distinguishing very sharply between such derivational suffixes as fall into small structures of vocalic gamuts and consonantal clusters and such others as are entirely isolated. It turns out that only the former category shows any impressive degree of productivity. If the small-scale experiment here undertaken is judged successful, I expect to apply the new approach to diachronic soundings-in-depth and eventually to extend it to distinctly larger slices of material.

My active curiosity about Asturo-Leonese has now lasted over more than a quarter-century. It was originally sparked by my dual commitment to the study and teaching of Peninsular Spanish and Portuguese, between which the Asturo-Leonese cluster of dialects forms a transitional zone and, in certain respects, represents an intermediate type. With the passage of time I have become more responsive to those features and ingredients of Asturo-Leonese that are truly original and solicit study for their own sake rather than to the elements that form a bridge between the two powerful neighbors. My first group of pertinent publications stretches from the early 'forties to the mid-'fifties and includes two notes (Language, XIX, 256-258, and XXV, 437-446) and three book reviews—two of them of rather ambitious size (Language, XXIII, 60-66; XXV, 291-307; XXX, 128-153). After a break, which I now deeply regret, I have recently reverted to the entertaining sets of problems posed by this family of dialects; see my diachronically slanted article, dedicated to the memory of Ramón Menéndez Pidal, in the April 1969 issue of Hispanic Review ("The Five Sources of Epenthetic /j/ in Western Hispano-Romance: A Study in Multiple Causation")—a piece which transcends the geographic limits of Cabraniego, but, nevertheless, places a premium throughout on that subdialect so inexhaustibly rich in solvable puzzles.

It remains for me to record my special gratitude to three persons: first, to Professor Percival B. Fay for his meticulously careful critical reading of the entire manuscript, with heightened attention to matters of formulation; second, to my friend Diego Catalán Menéndez-Pidal, for his uniquely expert technical bits of advice on miscellaneous particulars; and, third, to my junior friend Margaret Sinclair Breslin for her skill, encouragement, and cheerfulness in typing and helping me index the difficult material as well as for offering, in the process, numerous valuable suggestions which I have made it a point to heed.

Y.M.

Berkeley,
March 18, 1969

CONTENTS

INTRODUCTION

I

As a rule, Spanish dialect monographs heavily emphasize lexis at the
expense of grammar, and, within the narrow space reserved for the latter,
pay conspicuously scant attention to the mechanics of derivation and composition. In this respect, María Josefa Canellada's Madrid thesis dedicated
to one East-Central subdialect of Asturian ("El bable de Cabranes"; Suppl.
31 to Revista de Filología Española, Madrid, 1944) marks no exception to
the rule: The four pages or so (25-29) devoted to a bird's-eye view of miscellaneous problems of prefixation and, above all, suffixation do not begin to do
justice to the intricacies of the local patterns of word formation.[1]

[1] Of the five formal reviews which Canellada's thesis has elicited I have been unable to consult Carola Reig's in Mediterráneo (Valencia), II (1944), 272f. The short
piece by J. M. Alda Tesán in the Boletín de la Biblioteca de Menéndez Pelayo (San-
tander), XXI (1945), 96-98, is impressionistic and aimed at the general reader; the
side-remark on Arag. zafar-ache 'secluded stretch of water adjoining a river and
reserved for a catch of live eels' beside Sp. dial. zafar-eche, -iche 'pond, reservoir'
aptly illustrates vocalic gamuts pervading Romance suffixation, but has little bearing
on the book-review assignment. Despite its brevity H. Lausberg's delayed reaction
in Romanische Forschungen, LXIX (1953), 450f. is substantial; aside from attacking
a number of lexical problems the critic, focusing on derivation, pairs off - i e g u and
- i z u, draws attention to dimin. - u c u (nouns) and - u c a r (verbs)—conducive to the
preservation of such links between p e l - a r and p e l - u c - a r 'to pick, pluck' (ears
of wheat, flowers) as have been blurred elsewhere—and contrasts dimin.-derog.
- a s c u in Asturian with Sp. -astro. The most detailed of all assessments was con-
tributed by F. Krüger in the Anales del Instituto de Lingüística (Mendoza, Prov. of
Cuyo, Argentina), IV (1950), 267-275; most of the reviewer's remarks are lexical or
syntactic, with frequent side-glances at material civilization, but one can ferret out
a few telling comments on derivational suffixes, e.g., on those used in diminutives
(p. 268) and on - a t u (pp. 270, 273). The fifth book review was my own, in Language,
XXIII (1947), 60-66. One statement in it, concerning the distribution of -o and -u (see
p. 63), aroused the interest of W. von Wartburg; see that scholar's Die Ausgliederung
der romanischen Sprachräume (Bern, 1950), p. 14.

Canellada's monograph was one of several subjected to scrutiny by M. L. Wagner
in his article—valuable despite its unfortunate polemic slant—"Etymologische Rand-
bemerkungen zu neueren iberoromanischen Dialektarbeiten und Wörterbüchern,"
Zeitschrift für romanische Philologie, LXIX (1953), 347-391; cf. my rejoinder in

Yet the roughly three and a half thousand words recorded by the author constitute an interesting slice of material inviting both descriptive and historico-comparative analysis. Phonetically, the author (a student and, later, associate of A. de Lacerda) is one of the best-trained Spanish field-workers, particularly as regards the analysis of pitch contours, and her field-notes, in addition to the reliability of the transcription,[2] seem to be adequate on the side of definitions (verbal and, in part, pictorial: sketches and photographs) and occasional exemplifications. The editing, on the other hand, has been done in a very slipshod fashion, especially with respect to cross-referencing;[3] also, Canellada's book shares with other Madrid disser-

Romance Philology, IX (1955-56), 50-68, and Wagner's rebuttal in Romanische Forschungen, LXVIII (1956), 443-450, as well as the critical obituary in Romance Philology, XVI (1962-63), 281-289, reproduced in Portraits of Linguists, ed. T. A. Sebeok (Bloomington and London, 1966), II, 463-474. Many lexical data collected by Canellada were later absorbed by A. Zamora Vicente (her husband) into the semanti-cally arranged word lists of his own monograph, Léxico rural asturiano: palabras y cosas de Libardón (Colunga) (Granada, 1953), passim, and not a few have been used by the team of younger Peninsular dialectologists.

[2]In her introductory sketch (pp. 7-66), separated by three plates from the vocabu-lary proper, the author has recourse to narrow phonetic transcription, as established for the Madrid School, around 1918, by T. Navarro Tomás. In the Glossary itself (pp. 69-372) the entries appear in boldface, while for the purpose of cross-references and for enhanced authenticity of certain ingredients of definitions, italics are pressed into service, with standard spelling favored (except for the use of x for /š/) and with b symbolizing, phonemically, both [b] and [β]; d, analogously, matching both [d] and [δ], etc., while z and c before front vowel, distributed in conventional manner, both serve to represent the same phoneme /θ/. For the sake of convenience I have, in general, adopted this spelling, despite its lame compromises, even to the use of c u a for /kwa/, since it has been adhered to by the authors of several dialect monographs, except that I separate by a hyphen the reflexive pronoun from certain infinitives. In the original, stereotyped phrases and sentences cited under some entries appear in roman, enclosed by guillemets; I have here omitted the latter and spaced out all dialect forms; cf. n. 7, infra.

[3]Errors of this kind, attributable to haste and carelessness, mar almost every page. In her Introduction, Canellada adduces a p a l p a r (8); (p a l o m b u) t u r c a z (12); l l e g r e , l l o b u , n i ñ í n , and p o b r i q u í n (13), all of which are omitted from the Glossary, while m a n t i q u í n is found only s.v. m a n t e and the closest diminu-tive from pequeño actually recorded is p e q u e r r i ñ í n . The same degree of incon-sistency detracts within the bounds of the Glossary itself from the value of numerous cross-references, a feature which, given tidier execution, might have made that Glossary remarkably helpful, as are indeed its pervasive references to drawings and photographs. It would be tedious to point out in detail other shortcomings of the book, such as the author's failure to identify and characterize her informants (except for one fleeting remark on p. 10, n. 2); to describe the specific conditions under which

tations of the last quarter-century one irremediably serious shortcoming:
Its collection of dialect words is confined to those departing from standard
Spanish usage in more than trivial ways.[4] Assuming that the chosen dialect
has given rise to a group of noteworthy derivatives (say, diminutives) un-
paralleled in Castilian, one can again and again make at best educated guesses
about the local survival of the corresponding primitives, many if not all of
which the dialect may happen to share with the standard, the result being that
they have remained unrecorded.[5] I have tried to make it plain to the reader
which primitives have been extrapolated rather than discovered in the actual
record.

The very tentative study here offered is descriptive, though not to the point
of absolute exclusion of incidental genetic considerations. Comparison and
reconstruction of events have, however, been rigorously kept apart from
description and have, on purpose, been indulged in rather parsimoniously;
whenever possible, I try to visualize derivatives not as stemming from primitives, but as coexisting with them, a preference which has, for once, led to
the deliberate neglect of petrifacts, despite their undeniable usefulness in
reconstructions. The time has not yet come to offer a fully developed sketch
of Asturo-Leonese suffixal derivation in diachronic perspective, not even one
conceived on the scale of A. Kuhn's thorough but less than exhaustive study
of analogous conditions in Upper Aragonese.[6] The aim of this short mono-

---

the recording was carried out; to explain recurrent abbreviations (A. stands for
Acevedo and Fernández, R. for A. de Rato y Hevia); and to prepare herself adequately
for the task on the side of Latin (a single slip will serve to exemplify·her deficient
workmanship: She seems to assume that the sequence -UND- underlies e s c o n d o
and r e s p o n d o [12]).

[4]On this point it suffices to draw attention to D. Catalán Menéndez-Pidal's scathing
strictures embodied in his authoritative review of a Western Asturian monograph (1954)
from the pen of L. Rodríguez-Castellano (see Romance Philology, IX [1955-56], 367-
370), as well as to B. Bloch's pungent editorial comment in Language, XXIII (1947), 65.

[5]Thus, one learns about the semantically intriguing pair b e n t - á n and - a n u ,
but can only guess that b e n t a n a 'window' is used as well; from t r i g (u) - í n
'clearly perceptible wheat-flavor in the bread' one infers that t r i g - u 'wheat' is
very much alive, and every bit of collateral and indirect evidence supports this surmise, but the author makes no explicit mention of t r i g u , etc.

[6]See the separate section reserved for word-formation (pp. 158-245) in his Habili-
tationsschrift "Der hocharagonesische Dialekt," Revue de linguistique romane, XI
(1935), 1-312, and numerous relevant passages in the shorter companion piece, "Der
lateinische Wortschatz zwischen Garonne und Ebro," Zeitschrift für romanische
Philologie, LVII (1937: Karl Jaberg Festschrift), 326-365. The relatively most searching, if brief, treatment of Asturo-Leonese derivation has come from P. Sánchez Se-
villa, "El habla de Cespedosa de Tormes," Revista de filología española, XV (1928),
131-172, 244-282, esp. 155f. and 164-172 (the author operates with "falsos afijos y
prefijos").

graph, then, is to delve into a little-known field and, in the process, to experiment with a new technique (see infra).

The paper falls into three parts. Part One examines certain methodological preliminaries to the following classification, e.g., the relation of suffixes to interfixes, on the one hand, and to suffixoids as well as to suffixal increments and augments, on the other. Part Two, the core of the entire venture, is a catalogue of the suffixes, characterized by one analytical innovation: Whereas it has hitherto been customary, at least in Romance quarters, to classify derivational suffixes either on the basis of their pillar consonant(s): k, p, f, -ng-/-nk-, etc. or, alternatively, on the basis of their function, i.e., their ability to generate mass-nouns, abstracts, agentives, iteratives, diminutives, hypocorostics, etc., an attempt has here been made, presumably for the first time, to segregate such suffixes as show a single form (e.g., -ura which is not flanked by *-ara, *-era, *-ira, *-ora, let alone by *-iera, *-uera, *-ueyra) from others which appear in pairs or clusters, such as -án, -ín, and -ón; -aco, -ico, and -uco, and the like. The separate study of the latter may allow the analyst to concentrate his attention on both the pillar-consonants and the preceding vowels, which jointly form a highly idiosyncratic structural "grid." An approach so slanted may lead to such questions as these: Does the existence of /t/ and /k/ as consonantal pillars create an "empty case" for /p/, a vacuum which clamors for appropriate remedy? In case the vowel-gamut is short, as when only -al and -il can be subsumed under the L-pillar, does one sense the speakers' predisposition to fill the "empty slots" by groping for the absorption of -el, -ol, and -ul words? Can one extrapolate a common semantic denominator for the i's of -icu, -ín, -iñu, -ixu, -izu, etc.? Part Three embodies a succinct summary of the major results obtained and, by way of counterview, highlights those facts which may, on some future occasion, qualify for an imaginative diachronic treatment of the same material.

II

As background information a few words may be in order regarding the district ("concejo") of Cabranes. It lies, sprawling over hilly terrain, in the County ("partido judicial") of Infiesto—which, in turn, is located in the Province of Oviedo—and numbered, a quarter-century ago, over 4,000 speakers, a figure that, one gathers, must be revised upwards. The "concejo" comprises a few hamlet-sized parishes ("parroquias"), of which the largest, Santolaya (or, more formally, Santa Eulalia de Cabranes), serves as its administrative center, plus a number of loosely scattered farmhouses ("caseríos"). At the time the field work was carried out, no railways and no major highways intersected the district, and it was secluded by massive mountain chains from eastern and southern neighbors. The culturally all-important frontier against the south (which means against Castilian influence) is further accentuated by a river, a railway, and a highway jointly flanking the district. The population—one would assume it to be for the most part illiterate, though Canellada (to be known, henceforth, as "the author") is bashfully inexplicit on this point except for mentioning widespread superstitions—survives almost entirely on agriculture and cattle-raising, producing maize, potatoes, apples, and spelt, all four strictly for domestic consumption, and selling cattle, cider, as well as dairy products at the weekly market in near-by Infiesto.

In this relatively isolated and idyllic area numerous archaisms have, as one would expect, been preserved, a feature heavily emphasized by Canellada, perhaps at the expense of the dialect speakers' equally remarkable creativity, earthy humor, and vividness of imagination. As regards lateral pressures, it would seem that the subdialect of Cabranes was originally close to Eastern Asturian centered around Villaviciosa (a variety by now well known through the research of B. Vigón and his successors), and that it was weaned away from this association through the growing influence of Central Asturian raying out from the provincial capital of Oviedo—the closest urban area. These two links have, in turn, been increasingly eroded through the irresistible impact of Castilian, especially on the younger generation. The field-worker has observed younger folk conversing in standard Spanish with Asturian ("bable") pitch (p. 10)—just as the younger German Swiss now succeed in mastering standard German at present—but the symbiosis, I find, extends to lexicon and grammar as well, including, as one would predict, patterns of derivation. Then again, one comes across words which through some such telltale feature as the absence of an intervocalic -l- or -n- betray their cradle somewhere near the Atlantic Coast. For all their significance, these dynamic or diffusional aspects of the Cabranes variety of Asturian must recede into the background in this particular sketch, geared to straight description rather than to the reconstruction of events.[7]

[7]In the following text (and, occasionally, in this Introduction) I space out forms —including mere segments of words—recorded in Cabranes; underline other specimens of Romance material; and use capitals for Latin bases.

PART ONE
PRELIMINARY CLASSIFICATORY PROBLEMS

110. Neutralization of hierarchy.

For a genuine derivational relationship between two units to prevail, it is ordinarily necessary that primitive (= P) and derivative (= D) be simultaneously present in the given speech community. In borderline cases a word may qualify for the status of a quasi-derivative even in the absence of a primitive, provided, first, its final segment coincides in shape with a neatly detachable derivational suffix and, second, its total meaning fits smoothly into the pertinent series of genuine derivatives.

In exceptional instances, however, the derivational hierarchy may be completely neutralized in the synchronic perspective. Thus, on the one hand it is possible in Asturian to extract a radical-stressed action noun either in -u (masc.) or in -a (fem.), or even a pair of such nouns, from practically any verb, esp. if that verb has an -ar infinitive. The initial relationship between verb (P) and noun (D) is blurred if the original action noun is allowed to extend or to shift its meaning (typically, in the direction of 'place,' 'tool,' 'pile'). On the other hand, verbs, again especially those in -ar, can be freely derived from nouns, regardless of meaning; most of the eligible nouns in this reversal of roles between P and D happen to end in -u or -a. Consequently, there is, for the speaker—and for the descriptive analyst—no telling whether tosquila 'shearing' (cf. the figurative phrase dar una tosquila 'to administer a spanking') is hierarchically subordinate to tosquilar 'to give a haircut to, shave (close), crop, shear,' or vice versa, though the language historian may supply an answer from his vantage point. Comparable cases of suspended or neutralized hierarchy include the following pairs: cabruñar 'to hone a scythe, hitting it with a hammer on an anvil' beside cabruñu 'honing' (a scythe), 'sharp edge' (of a scythe); llebantar 'to raise, lift' beside llebantu 'raising, lifting';[8] mag-ostar, -ustar 'to roast chestnuts'

[8]Canellada lists llebante as a rival postverbal from lle-bantar, citing as sole example tá'l tiempu de llebante 'está el tiempo con tendencia a levantar.' I am rather reminded of the cognate Sp. levante 'levanter' (wind); cf. the phrase de levante 'ready to leave.'

[6]

beside f a c e r m a g ü e s t u 'to engage in chestnut-roasting'; m a s u ñ a r
'to handle, finger, fiddle with' beside m a s u ñ u 'handling, etc.'

111. Acephalous word families.

Where no primitive can be readily identified, the "feeling" for a derivational relationship is kept at a peak if there coexist two or more such formations as give the impression of constituting derivatives. Thus, the rivalry,
within the narrow confines of Cabranes, between l l i m - a z and - i a g u
'snail' and the separate occurrence of - a z and - (i) a g u in approximately
comparable contexts sharpens the speakers' awareness of the radical *l l i m -,
even if it is not found in isolation. The existence of coll. Sp. calamorr-a
'head' alongside -ada 'butt' (with the head) and -azo 'bump' (on the head)
prepares us to expect Ast. c a l a - m u r n i a. Canellada fails to include
such a word, but does list c a l a m u r n i - a z u, - ó n 'strong knock on the
head,' two items which virtually guarantee the existence—at the very least,
the intelligibility—of such a primitive. Similarly, b e r r - a c u 'ill-tempered
man,' b e r r - í a 'sheep in rut' probably vindicate the presupposition of
* b e r r - on a certain level of consciousness; it is problematic whether
b e r r - i o n d u, locally defined as 'flavor acquired by such fruits or seeds
as have already germinated,' falls synchronically within the same family,
as historically it does beyond the shadow of a doubt, with a widely discrepant
meaning (Sp. verriondo 'rutting'). In fact, it seems likelier that b e r r - ó n
'he who lows, bellows, screeches' and b e r r o s 'bellowing' are associated
with b e r r - a c u and - í a, to which they are genetically linked (Lat. VERRĒS
'wild boar'), while b e r r ó n 'tadpole' seems to stand apart.

112. The radical.

In delimiting the r o o t - m o r p h e m e, the analyst will, of course, take into
account the typical Spanish stress-controlled alternation of e and ie, o and
ue, which Asturian, incidentally, enforces far less sharply than does Castilian.
But the liberalization of the concept "radical" may go much farther. Consonantal metathesis, for instance, should be no barrier to classing c a l a n -
i e g a 'irrigation ditch' with canal, provided the latter has locally remained
in use (of this we have no assurance) and as long as no semantic differentiation has ensued. If b a l a g a r stands for 'cone-shaped heap of grass on a
meadow,' the corresponding verb ('to form such heaps, pile up') should, if
normal, have been * e m - b a l a g a r - a r, but happens to be e m - b a l a g - a r,
through the agency of haplology. Since this pattern of compression is in all
likelihood not restricted to just one example, there is no need to deny e m -
b a l a g - a r (verb) the status of a derivative; one is free to list the underlying

root morpheme as (free form) b a l a g a r / (bound form) b a l a g -. As a
result of a very old sound shift (fronting and assimilation of Lat. K before
front vowels), Hispano-Romance offers copious examples of the alternation
of radical-final k̲ : z̲ (cf. OSp. v̲e̲z̲ 'time' : v̲e̲g̲a̲d̲a̲ 'id.,' Sp. p̲e̲r̲d̲i̲z̲ 'partridge'
: p̲e̲r̲d̲i̲g̲ó̲n̲ 'young partridge'). Through preservation of v̲e̲g̲a̲d̲a̲ and suffixal
elaboration on v̲e̲z̲, the Cabranes dialect uses b e g - a d a and b e z - o n a
as interchangeable synonyms, even in specific phraseological contexts:
(a l l á   u n a)   b e g a d a   =   b e z o n a 'some time, on some suitable occasion'
(in the indefinite future); the radical should be defined as b e z - / b e g -.
B e r - i c i u / [- θj] as a by-form of b e r - i z u / [-θ] 'heath(er); any back-
woods plant that can be nibbled' (cf. Sp. b̲r̲e̲z̲o̲) is inconspicuous, involving
just the familiar parasitic /j/, see Section 214.4; the structure of b e r i é n z -
a n u 'finer class of heather, with an extra-small flower' is obscured by (1)
the addition of the "unstressed suffix" - a n u (cf. Section 114); (2) the anticipatory epenthesis of the nasal; and (3) the—analogical?—substitution of i̲e̲
for i̲ (cf. Section 114). Nevertheless, so long as a common meaning holds
these three forms together, b e r i c (i) - and b e r i e n z - may be viewed as
allomorphs of a single root morpheme.

   One of the haziest features of Central Asturian structure is the interplay
of diphthong and monophthong in suffixal derivatives. Fundamentally, one
expects a rising diphthong (i e,   u e) in a tonic syllable, matched by a monophthong (e,   o) in a pretonic syllable; but there has been a tendency for the
diphthong to invade all members of a given word-family, with the result that
in some instances free alternation prevails, e.g., p (i) e s - c - a l or - a r
'peach-tree' beside p i e s c u 'peach,' t (i) e r r - a r 'to fill up a sinking terrain with earth' beside t i e r r a; while in others the spread of the diphthong
has apparently been standardized, e.g., r e - p o s t - i e g - a r 'to answer
grumblingly' beside r e - p o s t - i e g - u 'saucy, given to snapping back.' The
impact of this idiosyncrasy of Asturian varies according to whether D is a
noun (or adjective) or a verb, regardless of the form class of P. In the former
eventuality, the jolt is stronger, since no stem alternant appears, cf. Sp.
m̲i̲e̲m̲b̲r̲o̲ 'member, limb' beside m̲e̲m̲b̲r̲-u̲d̲o̲ 'burly, husky' as against C.-Ast.
m i e m b r u vs. m i e m b r - u d u. Conversely, in the case of a denominal
or de-adjectival verb it must be remembered that the radical-stressed forms
of its paradigm at all times shared the primitive's diphthong, so that one
simply witnesses the extension of one stem variant at the expense of another
within the same conjugational system, as in o r - i e l l - a r 'to circle or sur-
round at the edges,' 'start working from the edges,' beside o r - i e l l a 'border,
margin,' - i e l l u 'sharp edge' or in r e s t - i e l l - a r 'to card flax or wool
with a board dotted with iron nails' known as r e s t - i e l l u, - i e l l a.

113. Suffixoids.

Where no allowances can be made for privileged treatment (see Section
111, supra), many formations which the language historian is in a position
to decompose into smaller units, with special reference to an earlier evolutionary stage, will be treated by the descriptivist as indivisible wholes. Thus,
b e r i y a 'strength and vitality of babies' and b i d a y a 'temple' are, strictly
speaking, monomorphemic, even though their Latin prototypes, VIR-ĪLIA
(n. pl.) and VĪT-ĀLIA—amalgamated with the Celtic ancestor of Sp. brío?
—were clearly bimorphemic. The chief factors that make us reluctant to
class b e r i y a and b i d a y a as ordinary derivatives are, first, the unavail-
ability of a primitive *b e r - ; second, the functional haziness of - i y a and
- a y a even in those contexts where they demonstrably perform the duties of
genuine suffixes; third, the (relative) semantic remoteness of 'temple' from
the extant primitive b i d a 'life'; and fourth, the referential simplicity of
'temple,' which, as an anatomical term, flanks 'nose,' 'mouth,' 'neck,' 'liver,'
etc., and is not on a par with such complexly structured semantemes as
'breeder of beavers,' 'hiding-place of wolves,' 'tree producing chestnuts,'
'pear-shaped apple,' and the like.

In certain analyses, there may nevertheless be some point in bracketing
such word-final segments as have the appearance of a derivational suffix
(and diachronically, in most instances, represent traces of just such a suffix)
with authentic instances of derivation. The main reason for this classificatory
leniency is that a tenuous associative thread continues to link these splinters
to the main body of suffixal formations. The word-final segment so isolated
may well be labeled a "suffixoid."

114. Suffixal and suffixoid increments.

Gauged by their function, Romance derivational suffixes, in general, and
those of the Cabranes subdialect of Central Asturian, in particular, can be
divided into three categories: (1) They may serve to transpose a given root
morpheme from one form class to another (type: 'ugly' → 'ugliness'); (2) They
may produce, within the same form class, a new word, typically one with an
enriched, more complex referential value, e.g., 'maker or seller of . . .,'
'lair, nest, warren, abode of . . . '; (3) They may nuance the given word, indu-
cing the listener to wonder at, delight in, abhor, or disdain the shape or size
or smell of the object evoked ('big, tiny, cute, sweet, coarse, ugly . . . ').
Appendages to a word stem which fail to serve unequivocally any of these
three neatly distinguishable purposes do not, as a rule, qualify as derivational
suffixes—at least not in Romance.

There does exist, however, in Hispano-Romance a peculiar family of appendages to nouns—increments which stand apart formally in that, unlike the authentic suffixes, they fail to carry the main word stress; and which likewise form a group sui generis semantically, in that they perform none of the services just specified. One may designate them provisionally "suffixal augments or increments"; they are particularly plentiful in Asturo-Leonese. It is customary to set them off by the consonant which constitutes their central pillar (say, -g-, -l-, -n-, or -r-). The vowel preceding that consonant is well-nigh obligatorily a, and the final vowel is either -a or -u —not -e or zero—according to the gender of the primitive.

A relatively transparent case is that of a b i é s p - a r a 'wasp,' for which near-by varieties of Asturian use a b i e s p a , the equivalent of Sp. avispa; the proximity of a b i e s p a to Cabranes is dramatized by the continued existence there of the verb a b i e s p á - s e 'to get restless' [lit. 'behave like a wasp']. Where no contour of a primitive emerges from derivational surgery, one can at best posit a suffixoid increment, e.g., l l á b a n a 'any big, smooth-surfaced stone, esp. one used in the stove to bake cake.'

The situation can be complicated by the interplay of augment and deliberate distortion (taboo); in d e m ó n g - a n u (= W.Ast. -aro) 'devil' the intrusive velar must be charged to deliberate camouflage. From such starting-points a certain predilection for -ng- may well have been developed, allowing m i r u é n - g - a n u to coexist with better-rooted ´- n d a n u 'skinny child.' (D. Catalán inclines to recognize in -ng- a trace of the primitive's final [ŋ] segment; cf. Zeitschrift für romanische Philologie, LXXXII [1966], 483 f.)

Again, the rising diphthong of a b i é s p a r a , in which the historian may recognize merely an incidental feature, seems to have grown, for the dialect speakers, into a characteristic companion trait. This ie and, true to the users' leanings toward symmetry, its counterpart ue appear in the least expected contexts. Thus the local words for 'heather' (= Sp. brezo) are b e r i - z u and - c i u , but a better class of 'heather' will be referred to as b e r i é n z a n u , with anticipation of the nasal by way of additional amplification.[9] Thanks to the simultaneous intrusion of this trend and of a metaphor, m i r á n d a n u 'fraise des bois' is flanked by m i r u é - n d a n u , - n g a n u 'skinny child' (see supra). A few miles from Cabranes the 'heap of hay left drying in the meadow' is no longer known as b a l a g a r , but as either m a g ü e t u or, more relevant, b e r g ü é t a n u . The relation of m a - to b e r - invites a historical excursus (blend of two words facilitated by the inherent affinity

---

[9]This is one of the exceedingly rare word-pairs displaying a slight degree of semantic differentiation, which, in all likelihood, here represents a secondary, supervenient phenomenon.

of b- and m- ?), which cannot be supplied here; but the reappearance of u e
before - (t)anu is worth observing. (In this context the diphthong of Ast.
oriéganu as against Arag. orígano and Sp. orégano 'wild marjoram,' from
ORĪGANU, loses some of its outlandishness.)

The background against which these formations must be viewed is the
speakers' general delight in proparoxytones, an attitude which has presided
over their choice of táladru 'drill, auger' as against Sp. taládro, from
Celto-Lat. TARATRU, and which has led them to exploit opportune semantic
extensions (sábadu ~ sabad-iegu 'kind of sausage') and morphological
elaborations (sábanu 'small bed-sheet, made of coarse cloth,' an innovation produced from sábana). The concurrent preference for the vowel /a/
in the penultimate is illustrated by trébades 'trivet,' as against Sp. trébedes,
marked by a more etymological choice of vowels (TRIPEDĒS). The subtle
interplay of diphthong in the stressed and of /a/ in the following intertonic
syllable is dramatized by the fact that, where the intertonic vowel happens
to be other than /a/, no diphthong dominates the stressed syllable even if
one might have been expected to develop or to survive: cf. pértigu 'part
of a wagon' (despite OSp. piértega 'pole, rod' < PERTICA), alongside perteg-
al or pertigu-era 'place where potential rods are growing' (typically a
hazel grove), perteg-ón 'staff used for knocking down chestnuts.' A parallel
symptom of the extreme popularity of this accentual pattern and its phonologi-
cal and morphological correlates is the liveliness of lexical blends observable
in this particular domain; thus, pámpana abaxo 'with the mouth down-
ward' and pámpana arriba 'with the mouth upward' clearly involve papa
'chin' (cf. Sp. pap-ad-illa 'flesh under the chin,' also pap-ada 'double chin,
dewlap' playfully contaminated by inferrable pámpanu 'tendril, vine leaf.'
As early as 1891 A. Rato y Hevia recorded visibly facetious a la pamp-
an-eta 'carelessly, in a carefree way' (= Sp. a la bartola).

Of the various augments, the one characterized by the N clearly predomi-
nates in Cabranes; to the above-cited examples add en-truéz-anu 'fat
adhering to the tripe,' pínf-anu (= botiellu) 'stomach,' táng-ana
beside tanga 'kind of blood pudding,' and tuérz-anu 'device, involving
two sticks placed crosswise, for suspending the chains of the hearth,' clearly
a satellite of torc-er 'to twist, bend, turn'; I assume that en-truéz-anu
presupposes *en-tuérz-anu. It is further plausible that the same ´-anu,
no longer clearly distinguishable from -ánu, enters as an interfix (see
Section 115, infra) into such formations as pic-an-iellu 'woodpecker'
(= pic-urr-inch-ón, picucerb-al; cf. Sp. pico) and ping-an-exu,
ping-an-eta 'gutter, pipe of a drying-up fountain,' cf. Sp. ping-ar 'to drip.'

115. Interfixes.

The term "interfix" is currently in wide use among Romance linguists as the designation of that segment, typically devoid of any clearly circumscribed meaning and in many instances serving no immediately recognizable purpose, which appears wedged in between the radical and the word-final derivational suffix—as a rule, semantically and grammatically well-defined.[10] In dissecting Ast. dulc-er-ina 'small, very sweet cherry,' one can argue that dulc-/dulθ/ is the radical, -ina the familiar diminutive and individuating derivational suffix, and -er- a rather nondescript ingredient which, depending on the observer's angle, separates the two or mediates between them. In descriptive and genetic analysis alike, there exist alternatives to operating with interfixes. Thus, it is theoretically permissible to posit two, or even three, forms of the radical, dulc(e) as the free form and as the kernel of, say, dulz-ura 'sweetness' (assuming that abstract exists in our subdialect) and dulcer- as the bound form underlying dulcer-ina, cf. Germ. Geburt(s)-, Tod(es-), and the like. Another way of eliminating interfixes from one's morphological inventory is to assume the existence of a shorter suffix -ina and of a longer by-form ("suffix-chain") -erina; the consistent adoption and subsequent generalization of this procedure might swell the roster of suffixes by several hundred items. Considerations of numerical economy, structural tightness, and even esthetics counsel the recognition of interfixes or concatenators as clearly delimited, autonomous units.

The lexicon of the subdialect of Cabranes is replete with interfixes; here are a few samples:

(a) -AD-: rab-ad-al, -iella 'uropygium (of bird's body)' beside rab-al 'id.' (and, one assumes, rab-u 'tail'), cf. Sp. rab-ad-illa; de seg-ad-ín '(meadow) whose grass has been mowed' beside seg-añu (also -ón, -ote) 'small scythe,' seg-au 'supply of grass mowed';

[10]The term "interfix," proposed by H. Lausberg almost casually, in a book review, received its formal presentation in my lengthy article "Los interfijos hispánicos: problema de lingüística histórica y estructural," Miscelánea A. Martinet: Estructuralismo e historia, II (La Laguna, 1958), 107-199, and was later adopted by F. González Ollé, Los sufijos diminutivos en castellano medieval (Madrid, 1962), cf. J. R. Craddock's weighty review article, "A Critique of Recent Studies in Romance Diminutives," Romance Philology, XIX (1964-65), 286-325. I briefly reexamined the core, if not the ramifications, of the problem in my "Genetic Analysis of Word Formation," in Current Trends in Linguistics, ed. T. A. Sebeok, III: Theoretical Foundations (The Hague, 1966), 305-364, esp. 318-321; among the reactions to this new formulation I should like to single out B. Migliorini's comments in the May 1968 issue of Current Anthropology, pp. 26-29, cf. my response, ibid., pp. 49f., as well as some remarks of Anita Katz Levy in her unpublished Univ. of Pennsylvania (1969) dissertation, "Factors in the Distribution of Suffixes in the Romance Languages," see pp. 35, 43, 46f., 53-56, and 194. Concatenator is a term launched recently by the talented Slavist M. Shapiro.

(b) -AL-: a la pañ-al-uca 'grabbing, scrambling' (= Sp. a la rebatiña), cf. a-pañ-uc-ar 'to grasp sth. many times, or many trifles at once,' presupposing the local dialectal use of Sp. a-pañ-ar 'to pick, seize';

(c) -AN-: pic-an-iellu beside picu 'woodpecker' (unless one interprets it, with D. Catalán, as *pic-añ-iellu; see pic-añ-ón, infra); ping-an-eta, -exu, as defined and discussed supra, in Section 114;

(d) -AND-: llab-and-era 'stone reserved for laundry,' 'wagtail' (directly associated with llab-ar 'to wash,' with short-circuiting of the underlying intermediate link traceable to LAVANDA);

(e) -AÑ-: peg-añ-osu 'sticky' (paralleling Sp. peg-aj-oso) beside a-p(i)eg-ar, ringed by self-explanatory derivatives in-ad-iegu, -ad-ura, -aízu, cf. Sp. peg-ar 'to stick'; pic-añ-ón 'itchy' (= comici-osu, reminiscent of Sp. comezón 'itch'); on a possible link to pic-an-iellu see supra, under (c);

(f) -AR-: es-cuall-ar-au 'cut very low in the neck' (= Fr. décolleté); llend-ar-ina (= llend-ad-ora) 'wagtail' alongside llend-ar 'to make sure the cattle do not leave the pasture-ground'; (mi)g-ar-itu 'piece of bread or cake' beside mig-aya 'crumb, bit' and mig-ollu 'bit, soft part of bread (cake, etc.),' in preference to cacophonous *migu-itu; a la pañ-ar-uca 'grabbing, scrambling' (= pañ-al-uca, see supra); pap-ar-au 'mouthful' beside pap-au 'swallow' (cf. W.-Ast. pap-ar-ín, defined 'baby's pap' by Acevedo and Fernández);[11] peg-ar-ada 'covey of magpies,' -ata '[young?] magpie' alongside pega 'magpie,' peg(-ar-)-atu 'young of magpie'; salt-ar-icu 'unstable person,' lit. 'hopper,' beside salt-ad-era 'short outdoor ladder' (= pas-er-ina), salt-ona 'frog,' salta-praos 'grass-hopper' (lit. 'meadow-hopper'), the last-mentioned a compound displaying a slightly different kind of segmentation; seg-ar-eta 'song of the mowers' (?);[12]

(g) -ARR-: bey-arr-aes 'ways of old folk' beside biey-u 'old'; cag-arr-i-ón 'small plum, blue or black, disagreeable as to taste,' cf. Sp. cag-arr-uta 'cow or sheep dung'; pint-arr-ax-ar 'to daub,' conceivably an adaptation of Sp. pint-arr-aj-(e)-ar, flanks pintu 'spotted,' pinta 'freckle,' etc.;

[11] True, one may be tempted to circumvent the need for positing an interfix here by deriving paparau from pápar(a) 'pap.' Historically, the reverse sequence of events would be equally defensible.

[12] Listed as a synonym of the regionalisms an-, en-decha, of which the former was later left undefined and the latter altogether omitted.

(h) -AT-: l e n g u - a t - e r u 'foul-mouthed, garrulous';

(i) -AZ-: c o s t - a z - a d a 'nap,' unless directly related to c o s t -
a z u 'shoulder,' but cf. al r e - c o s t - í n 'on one's back,' a -, r e - c o s t -
i n - a r 'to carry on one's back'; p i n - a z - a d a 'heap (of money, etc.)'
beside p i n a 'wedge';

(j) -EG-/-IG-: p e d r - e g u - e r u 'stony path or place' beside
p e d r - e r u, - e r a 'id.'; p o d r - i g - a ñ u 'rotten substance (tree, fruit,
vegetable)' and - a ñ - á - s e 'to rot' beside p o d r - i z u 'stench due to
putrefaction'; (r e -) t o r c - i g - a ñ - a r 'to twist' beside t o r - c i ó n,
- z ó n 'cramp,' etc.;[13]

(k) -ER-: d u l c - e r - i n a 'small, sweet cherry' (see supra);
l l e c h - e r - i n a 'plant thriving amid grass, with yellow blossoms; its
stalk yields a white liquid' (from l l e c h e 'milk'); m e d -, m e l -,
m e m - e r - i z u 'song bird resembling the sparrow, with greenish feathers'
(from m i e l 'honey'?). Alternatively, the segmentation d u l c e - r - i n a
and l l e c h e - r - i n a could be advocated on the grounds that it exhibits
the mutual affinity between this interfix and the primitive's -e, in much
the same way as in standard Spanish the interfix /θ/, spelled c before
-ito, etc., and z before -uelo, etc., and primitives ending in -e are known
to attract each other, as in lotecillo 'small share,' from lote;

(l) -ERR-/-IRR-: apparently favored in nursery-style deriva-
tives ('wee, tiny'): p e q u - e r r - i ñ - í n; p o q u - e r r - i ñ - í n; with end-
less variations: p e q u - i r r plus - i ñ - í n, or - i c h - í n, or - i s q u - í n;
p i q u - i r r - i ñ - í n, etc.;

(m) -EST-: c o m - e s t - í n (noun and adj.) 'excessively lively,
restless, and meddlesome (person),' lit. 'devoured by restlessness' or
'having a gnawing appetite,' beside c o m e r 'to eat' (cf. Sp. com-est-
ibles 'edibles');

(n) -ET-: p r o b - e t - a y - u 'miserable, wretched,' a - p r o b - e t -
a y - a u 'looking impoverished,' beside p r o b e 'poor' (= Sp. pobre);

(o) -EX-: r a b - e x - i n a 'tantrum, conniption' (cf. Sp. rabi-eta,
Ptg. rab-ugem); r a b - e x - í u, - ó n, - u r a, even veiled r o b e x í u
'sour, impudent riposte,' presumably beside r a b i a 'fury';

(p) -IC-: (j u g a r a l a) p i e d r - i q u - i n a 'children's play with
pebbles,' beside p e d r - e r u 'path studded with stones,' p e d r - é s 'hard
(like stone),' etc.;

[13]The sequence - i g a ñ u may have split off from r a i g - a ñ u (= - ó n) 'root,
tree trunk torn out with its roots,' where - i g -, of course, forms part of the radical.

(q) -ICH-/-INCH-: pequ-irr-ich-ín 'tiny'; pic-urr-inch-ón 'woodpecker' (beside picu). Cf. Sp. berr-ench-ín 'grunt of angry boar,' 'rage, tantrum,' berr-inch-udo 'cross, irascible' and, in its wake, berr-inche 'rage, tantrum';

(r) -IN-: paxar-in-eta 'animal's milt, spleen' (= W.-Ast. paxar-ella), lit. 'little bird,' presumably beside páxa-ru;

(s) -ING-: per-ón and per-um-ing-ón ('pear-shaped'?) are identified as two local varieties of apples (p. 264, s.v. mazana). (An element -ing-, sometimes used in conjunction with other ingredients of undefined status and obscure provenience, occurs also in racy Spanish words, cf. voc-ing-l-ero 'loud-mouthed,' 'loquacious'; it enters into a neatly circumscribed set with -ang-, -eng-, -ong-, and has such identifiable suffixal equivalents as -enco, -engo;[14] but -ing- in this particular context could be -eg-/-ig- plus anticipatory nasal, as in -inch-, supra.)

(t) -IÑ-: poqu(-err-)iñ-ín 'tiny bit';

(u) -ISC-: pequ-irr-isqu-ín 'wee, tiny';

(v) -OL-/-UL-: mans-ol-ín 'hypocritically gentle,' no doubt used beside manso; pic-ol-iar 'to turn red' (speaking of cherries), lit. 'to be dotted with red spots' (?)—cf. pic-ar 'to knock sharply at the door,' etc.; pir-ul-iu 'small, red, very tasty plum' (cf. Sp. pera 'pear' and ciruela 'plum,' perhaps locally amalgamated). An infrequent interfix, with obvious links to -uelo and less obvious connections with -ueño, -oño;[15]

(w) -UR-: pig-ur-ada 'nap' (= cost-az-ada) beside pig-aciu (Rato y Hevia: pig-azu; Acevedo and Fernández: pig-a(r)zu, cf. pig-ac-iar 'to nod, slip to one side';

(x) -UZ-: (mazana) berd(uz)ona 'greenish apple'; cf. the Sp. suffix -uz(o), which forms a rather loose set with -az(o) and -iz(o);

(y) -Z-: This element, familiar from Sp. -z-uelo, -c-ete, etc., appears in Cabranes in porc-on-z-ón 'big hog,' fig. 'very dirty person,' where it serves as a wedge between two otherwise identical augmentative-pejorative -ón ingredients.

[14] I am unable to account for the -um- of per-um-ing-ón; as for the l of Sp. vocinglero, I would liken it to the optional, nonetymological -r- of the OSp. adverbial suffix -mient(r)e. In Hispano-Romance, adventitious l and especially r have been favored, in certain positions, as concluding elements of various consonant clusters. Historically, they do not represent residues of any identifiable morphemes.

[15] Does W.-Ast. mans-oño (Acevedo and Fernández) justify the reconstruction of *mans-oñ-ín, subject to consonant dissimilation at a later date?

For several reasons it seems advisable to separate this ensemble of occurrences from the (antihiatic) use of -g- in m i a g a r 'to meow' (= Sp. mayar or maullar). The bulk of interfixes so far surveyed are confined to nominal stems, to the exclusion of verbs, and have nothing to do with either sound symbolism or onomatopeia, which may have played a part in the shaping of m i a g a r .

It goes without saying that a truly sophisticated analysis of interfixes (based, to begin with, on an exhaustive inventory) would go far beyond providing a mere catalogue randomly organized, as illustrated by the samples just offered. The next steps would be for the analyst to assemble those items sharing a single consonant, or a consonant cluster ("pillar"), into neatly architectured series characterized by vocalic gamuts (the vowels at issue being those preceding the pillars); to determine whether such gamuts contain two, three, or more members and to probe the consequences of the gamuts' relative length or shortness; to compare the consonantal pillars structurally, on the basis of distinctive features, where a single consonant is involved, and, in addition, on the basis of the combinatory formulas presiding over the consolidation of consonant sequences into fixed groups, such as /sk/ or /nk/; to ascertain any denotation or connotation, or both, possibly attaching to each consonantal pillar as well as those peculiar to specific vowels, viewed both within each gamut and on a broader scale in a cross-gamut perspective; also, to identify all gaps, especially in the ranks of the pillar consonants. These are, essentially, the operations which, at the start, were announced for the tighter arrangement and closer inspection of stressed suffixes; they are equally applicable to the study of interfixes, a venture which, however, demands certain supplementary gambits on the part of the player, in as much as the interfixes, by definition accentually unstressed and semantically of light weight, depend in each instance distinctly more on their shifting environment than do heavily accented and, as a result, more autonomous derivational suffixes. Thus, given our recently increased knowledge of dissimilatory trends, we must, in this concluding phase of the breakdown, ask ourselves to what extent interfixes containing, say, l or r are influenced by the occurrence of laterals or vibrants elsewhere in the same word; where the supporting consonant cluster happens to contain a nasal, especially one placed before a velar or a prepalatal, as in Sp. vej-anc-ón 'decrepit' (= vej-arr-ón) and berr-ench-ín 'grunt of angry boar' or as in Ast. p e r - u m - i n g - ó n 'pear-shaped (apple),' the likelihood of ties—genetic and associative-synchronic—to -ac-, -ech-/-ich- and -eg-/-ig- invites exploration, as does the anticipatory insertion of a nasal provoked by word-terminal -ín or -ón. Finally, the specific relation of the vowel of the interfix to the vowel of the stressed suffix—in terms of mutual attraction or repulsion—deserves close attention. While incompatibilities between the stem vowel—placed typically in counterstress—and the suffix vowel is known to have led to compromises on either side of the dividing line, the vowels of interfixes are acoustically so weak and grammatically so unprotected that they can be expected to yield invariably to the pressures exerted by the suffix vowel and, on a minor scale, to those applied by the stem vowel, without producing any noticeable counterpressures.

120. Non-suffixal varieties of word-formation.

Although this paper is chiefly concerned with derivational suffixes, a brief glance at prefixation and composition seems imperative at this point, be it only on account of the fact that prefixes and suffixes are jointly pressed into service in parasynthesis, and of the further fact that the border line between composition and derivation is demonstrably quite fluid in Asturian.

121. Prefixation.

Like other varieties of Hispano-Romance, Asturian has a severely limited number of prefixes, which are essentially preverbs. These prefixes are practically the same as in Spanish, except for differences in range. Thus, d e - , which in Spanish appears only before /R/, as in de-rroc-ar 'to throw down from a rock' beside roca 'rock,' or else in patently learned formations (of the type de-medi-ar 'to divide in half, reach the middle of,' flanking medio 'half'), emerges in Cabranes before m - : d e - m o c - a r 'to cut or blunt an animal's horns,' refl. 'to lose its horns' (alongside m o c a / m o c h a 'hornless head of cattle'); d e m - o z - a r 'to sprout—speaking of Indian corn—with concurrent loss of the male blossom' (alongside m o z u 'eligible young man, fiancé').[16] Also, e s - , only vestigially preserved in Castilian (es-clar-ecer 'to brighten, light up, dawn' beside claro 'clear, bright, light'), is here

---

[16]To avoid morphotactic difficulties speakers will often insert -a- or -en-, occasionally -con- or some other intercalary element, between des- and the radical. These augments represent the prefixal counterpart of concatenators or interfixes. Examples: d e s - a - g a f - a r 'to alleviate an inflammation' (beside g a f u = e n - g a f - e n t - a u 'festering'); d e s - c o n - s o ñ - a r 'to awaken completely, dispel the last traces of sleepiness' (beside, one gathers, s u e ñ u); d e s - e n - u b - e l l - a r 'to wind or spool a tangled ball of yarn' (beside d u b - or u b - i e l l o , the counterpart of Sp. ovillo, and u b - i e l l - a r 'to make balls of yarn'). The process is fundamentally the same as the wavering, in English, between dis-sociate and dis-as-sociate, and there is no dearth of suitable models, such as d e s - a - g ü e y - a r 'to cure the evil eye' vs. a - g ü e y - a r 'to cast the evil eye' (g ü e y u 'eye'), d e s - e n - r (i) e s t r - a r 'to untie a string' beside e n - r i e s t r - a r 'to string cobs of maize, onions, etc., in order to expose them to the sun' (r i e s t r - a , - u 'string').

abundantly represented: e s - b o r o ñ - a r 'to crumble, break into pieces' matches b o r o ñ a 'ear of Indian corn'; e s - c a n d a n - a r 'to turn dry and skinny' accompanies c á n d a n u 'dry twig still attached to the tree.' Similarly, the use of t r e s - in the standard is sanctioned only where it means 'three': tres-dobl-ar 'to treble'; consequently, the process ranks as compositional rather than derivational. In regional Spanish, tres-quilar competes with tras- and es-quilar 'to shear,' occupying a borderline position among prefixes, since -quil-, though marginally recognizable as a unit (not unlike E. -ceive inferred from con-, re-ceive), fails to occur in isolation or to be endowed with any readily identifiable meaning. In the Cabranes dialect, t r e (s) - prevails over t r a (s) - : t r e - b e s - a r, favored for 'to traverse,' is not incompatible with t r a - b e s - ó n 'big, solid stick' (used, e.g., to bar a door or as part of the harrow)—one is left wondering whether Sp. re-vés 'reverse' is locally represented; t r e s - p a s - a r 'to cross over' presumably stands out sharply against paso 'step' and pasar 'to pass' (these two remain unmentioned).

As regards their semantic load, two prefixes, a - and e m - (e n -), are practically void, a loss of content which transmutes them into handy derivational tools (see infra), but not in the sense in which the other prefixes, loaded with a discernible meaning of their own, are useful to the speakers. C o m - (c o n -) appears in a variety of words, some of them easily decomposable: c o m - p o n - e d o r i u 'yeast' (beside p o n - e r 'to set,' etc.), c o n - f e c h - a r 'to break up (clods)' (beside f e c h - i s c u 'bad shape' and the p. ptc. f e c h u 'done, made,' cf. the sentence Canellada cites, p. 33),[17] but no central meaning emerges in this nucleus of transparent formations. Where c o m - (c o n -) happens to convey the expected message 'with, together,' the formations, ironically, are hard to dissect; cf. c o m - b a l e c h á - s e 'to conspire,' c o m - p a n g u 'pieces of meat, sausage, bacon thrown into the pot.' Still, a thin semantic thread linking c o n - c e y u 'council, evening party for dance and conversation' /c o n - c e y - a r 'to gather in the evening for games and gossip,' c o n - g r i ñ u 'wrapping' (fig. 'junk'), c o n - s i n t - i r 'to consent' probably suffices to hold together this crumbling group.

As is common in Hispano-Romance dialect speech, d e s - and e s - have become functionally indistinguishable ('un-, de-, dis-'), and there apparently prevails among them a measure of free alternation (cf. Canellada, p. 29); moreover, d e -, though far more meagerly represented, is neatly identifiable (see supra). Other more or less tidily contoured prefixes of severely

---

[17]On confechar/cohechar, a semantically and syntactically very difficult verb, see D. Catalán's article, "La pronunciación [ihante] por /iffante/ en la Rioja del siglo XI," Romance Philology, XXI (1967-68), 410-435, esp. 420-426.

limited scope are e n t r e - 'between': e n t r e - m e c - e r 'to mix, inter-
mingle,' e n t r e - (s) t a l l - a r 'to catch some one or sth. between two
objects' (cross of entre-tallar 'to cut between' and estallar 'to burst, ex-
plode'?); r e - : r e - l l a m b - é - s e 'to lick one's chops, relish' beside
l l a m b - e r 'to lick, eat candy' (for details see infra); s o b r e - 'over' :
s o b r e - l l e v - a r 'to weigh down on, make one lose one's balance' (speaking of excessive weights); s o - 'under': s o - l l i b i - a r 'to make the soil
soft, porous, fluffy' (hinting at toads and moles) beside l l i b - i a n u 'light-
weight' (adj.), 'lung' (n.) and l l i b - i e r u 'soft, fluffy' (in reference to the
soil), also s o - p e s - a r 'to test, try out the weight of an object by attempt-
ing to lift it; to grope,' presumably beside well-entrenched p e s u and p e s -
a r , and s o - l l o m b u 'sirloin'—minus the diminutive suffix of Sp. so-lom-
illo—beside l l o m b u 'back, ridge, loin'; t r e s - 'behind-' (see supra).[18]
The material on c o n t r a - 'counter-, against' is too scant to invite any
characterization of its status.

The more graphically suggestive a prefix, the better the chances of its
transfer to denominal formations. Significantly, there are no traces of a -
and e m - (e n -), both pictorially empty, performing such services; also,
c o m - (c o n -) is too hazily silhouetted on the semantic side to qualify for
such a role. Over against these gaps note s o b r e - m u r i u 'piece of wood
placed above the wall (= m u r i u)' and s o b r e - p é r t i g a 'part of the
wagon placed below [sic] the tongue' (= p é r t i g a),[19] also t r e s - l l u z
'glint, gleam, diffused light' (l l u z 'light'), t r e s - m o n t - o r i u 'huge
amount, pile, mountain of sth.'

P e r - as a preverb is used sparingly in Cabranes (at least, by Asturo-
Leonese standards), not infrequently in formations with similarly structured
Spanish counterparts (p e r - s i g u - i r 'to pursue' beside s i g u - i r 'to
follow,' cf. Sp. per-seguir/seguir) or with remote equivalents in Spanish
(p e r - c a n c i a r 'to manage to bring about'; cf. Sp. per-cance 'mischance,'
pl. 'perquisites' beside al-cance 'pursuit, reach, range' / al-canz-ar 'to
catch up with, overtake') or else with a Spanish cognate involving (learned)

---

[18]If p e l - e x a r 'to fight, struggle, wrestle, quarrel' exists, as is very likely (cf.
Sp. pel-ear), then s o - p e l - e x a r (= s o l - m e n a r) 'to shake, wave vigorously'
would be an additional example in point.

[19]The direction inherent in the meaning is puzzling. The confusion could have been
brought about by the different uses to which p é r t i g - a and p (i) é r t i g - u have been
put by carters; or s o b r e - has here, by way of exception, been used, especially before a p-, as one of the many by-forms of s o - , alongside s o l - and s o n - : s o l -
m e n a r 'to shake, wave energetically' and s o n - s a ñ a r 'to ape, mimic, imitate
mockingly'—neither of which may be any longer decomposable in Cabranes. On PER-
TICA see my article, "Latin PEDICA, *PĒNSUM, and PERTICA in Hispano-Romance,"
in Mélangers de philologie offerts à Alf Lombard, Études romanes de Lund, XVIII (1968),
130-150.

<u>pro-</u>: p e r - m e d i - a r 'to average.'[20] In addition, p e r - can be freely attached to most adjectival and to many adverbial qualifiers to form, at the start, facetious and, in the long run, ironic and rigidified superlatives (see Canellada, pp. 25 f.): p e r - a - f o r r - a u 'extra-cheap' [?] (i.e., 'exorbitantly expensive'), p e r - b l a n c u 'gleaming white' (i.e., 'black'), p e r - g ü e n u 'exceedingly good,' p e r - l l i m p i u 'clean as a hound's tooth,' p e r - l l o n g u 'startlingly long'; p e r - l l o ñ e 'far, far away,' etc.

R e - is rather sharply profiled, even though l l u g - a d a and r e - l l u g - a d a (d e s o l) are listed as being mutually interchangeable and are likened referentially to g ü e y - a d a 'glance, wink,' from g ü e y u 'eye.' Far more typical of the vigor of r e - in Hispano-Romance are r e - m o c - i c - a r 'to rejuvenate oneself, look and act young,' r e - m o l i n - a r 'to turn a wagon around' (a movement evoking the wing or paddle wheel of a mill), r e - s a l i b - a u (a synonym of l l a s p - a r d - e r u) 'very lively, gossipy, and prattling' (lit. 'spewing forth drops of spittle in repartee'), r e - t a y - a or - u 'scrap' (beside t a y - a 'cut, slice'), (r e) - t o r c - i g - a ñ - a r 'to twist around' (cf. t o r c - e r), r e - t r u c - a r 'to grumble, retort' (the implied 'exchange of insults' calls to mind Sp. <u>troc-ar</u> 'to barter' and, even more, <u>re-truc-ar</u> [in billiards] 'to kiss, hit again' [of a rebounding ball]): The recurrent ideas are, then, 'to return' (to a place or stage), 'to turn around,' 'to react, respond to a challenge,' 'to repeat an action, often many times, and carry out the design to perfection.' As in Spanish, one encounters the expanded variants r e s - : r e s - c o c - e r 'to chafe' (beside c o c - e r 'to cook, soften logs of wood by soaking them in water'), r e s - q u (i) e b r - a 'crack, split' (beside <u>quebr-ar</u> 'to break,' undoubtedly extant); and r e t a - : r e t a - f i l a 'line, string.'

In conjunction with and probably on account of the semantic emptiness of a - and e m - (e n -) the mobility of these elements is extreme, reminding one of the rhythmically ornamental character of the suffixal augments (see Section 114). This remark applies to primary verbs, where the occasionally observed mildly intensive overtone of the a - variant may represent but a secondary accretion : p a l p - a r 'to touch, grope through' beside a - p a l p - a r 'to touch repeatedly and purposefully.' The comment holds true even more cogently for denominal verbs, such as (a) - c o n - c e y - a r 'to forgather for an evening party' (c o n - c e y - u, lit. 'council'). There exist numerous models for a - c o n c - e y - a r, e.g., a - c u e r b - a r 'to caw or croak like a raven' (cf. c u e r b u), a - c u r (r) u x - á - s e 'to cover oneself, wrap up, bundle up so as to guard against chill' (cf. c o - , c u - r u x a 'screech owl,'

---

[20]On the background of this substitution see my article "The Ancient Hispanic Verbs <u>posfaçar</u>, <u>porfaçar</u>, <u>profaçar</u>: A Study in Etymology and Word-Formation," <u>Romance Philology</u>, III (1949-50), 27-72.

curuxu 'eagle owl'), a-tech-á-se 'to seek shelter under a roof' (cf.
techu 'house, roofed stockyard, etc.'), a-zurd-iell-ar 'to hit with a
lash' (cf. zurd-iell-u, -a 'lash'). There also exists a wealth of parallels
for con-cey-ar, e.g., madr-eñ-ar 'to clatter with wooden shoes' (pl.
madr-eñes), may-ar 'to crush, pound, grind,' 'to thresh' (wheat), 'to
mash' (apples, for cider), 'to break into pieces' (clods), 'to thrash' (one's
enemy's ribs) beside mayu 'wooden mallet or maul'; mes-ori-ar 'to
harvest wheat with two equal-sized, sharpened sticks' (pl. mes-ori-es).
Viewed against this background, the genetic filiation of con-cey-ar and
a-con-cey-ar may be formulated in several ways, but descriptively it
suffices to state that a- is here an unstable element, devoid of any identifiable meaning of its own. Prefixes other than a- and em- (en-) are
rarely dispensable to such an extent; but note cacipl-ar/(es)-cacip-
p(l)ar 'to entangle, upset things; gossip' beside cacip(l)-eru 'meddler,
tattler' and the phrase revolvé-se la cacípola 'not to feel in good
health.'

122. Parasynthesis and regression from parasynthesis.

In parasynthetic formations, e.g., in verbs generated by adjectives, a-
and em- (en-) seem to be, upon occasion, interchangeable: a-curt-
i-ar ~ en-curt-i-ar 'to shorten' beside curt-i-u 'short' (as
against Sp. either a-cort-ar/cort-o or em-bot-ar 'to blunt, dull' /bot-o,
en-cresp-ar 'to curl' / cresp-o). A- seems to be the favorite with
-yar, a combination distinctly more common in Asturian than in Spanish,
which latter, by way of closest approximation, offers (res)-quebr-aj-ar-se
'to crack, slit, split' beside quebr-aja 'fissure'; cf. in Cabranes a-trist-
ayar, -ayá-se 'to grow sad,' a-palp-ayaɪ 'to touch, grope' (at the
midpoint, as regards the degree of intensity, between a-palp-ar and
a-palp-uñ-ar). Though there is on record a sprinkling of inchoative
-ecer formations extracted from adjectives without any concomitant support from a prefix (maf-ec-er 'to turn moldy or musty,' maur-ec-er
'to ripen'), the typical disyllabic adjective in -o/-a generates an -ecer
verb with concurrent support from a-: a-choch-ec-er 'to become
doting, doddering' (choch-u), a-tenr-ec-er 'to soften up, make
tender' (tenr-u), a-toch-ec-er 'to stultify' (toch-u), a-tosqu-
ec-er 'to coarsen' (tosc-u). (On this point Spanish parts company
with Asturian, pairing off with -ecer, of all prefixes available, en- rather
than a-: en-tern-ec-er 'to move to pity,' en-tont-ec-er 'to make foolish or
silly,' en-torp-ec-er 'to benumb,' or else espousing the rival solution a-ar,
as in a-larg-ar 'to lengthen'; hence a-bland-ar ~ em-bland-ec-er 'to soften,

soothe,' a-grand-ar ~ en-grand-ec-er 'to enlarge,' while en-trist-ec-er 'to sadden' has completely evicted a-trist-ar; see Section 214.4, infra.

Through regression, an adjective, shedding in one gambit the parasynthetic verb's inflectional equipment and prefix, can become a new unit and a fresh center of attention (the classic example in Spanish is cuerdo 'sane, wise, prudent,' lit. 'one who remembers earlier experiences,' from a-, re-cord-ar 'to remember,' lit. 'to take to heart,' based in turn on L. COR, -DIS). How can a descriptivist establish this hierarchy without having recourse to cross-temporal evidence? The wider semantic spectrum, the higher incidence (provided statistical information is available), plus the richer accumulation and greater diversity of derivatives may jointly tend to assign to the verb the rank of a secondary formation, based on a deeply buried primary noun, while the adjective emerges from the assessment as tertiary in evolutionary role and, often, in synchronic status as well. Thus, Ast. c u e s t -u 'hanging, biased, slanted' seems founded on a-cost-ar 'to lean, list' (if that verb exists locally; only a - c o s t - a c i - a r , -a z a r / -i n - a r 'to carry on one's shoulder' are recorded) as well as on the lexical cluster r e - c o s t - i (y) - á - s e 'to lie down,' r e - c o s t - i n - a r 'to load on one's shoulder,' and a l r e -c o s t í n 'on one's back,' the whole in the last analysis based on Hispano-Romance cuesta 'hill, slope; back, shoulders.'

In analyzing a - z a p a t - a u 'hard fig growing out of season' (lit. 'shoe-shaped, shoe-like'—with a hint at its form or, more plausible, at the leathery hardness of skin and pulp?—D. Catalán reminds me of Sp. patatas zapateras, carne dura como suela de zapato), it is supererogatory to posit between the primitive z a p a t - u 'shoe' and the new qualifier a - z a p a t - a u an a - a r verb as an intermediate link, though such a verb remains an ever-present latent possibility.[21]

123. Compounds and semi-compounds.

Composition is used on a limited scale in Asturian, and the dialect of Cabranes displays no conspicuous departure from the general trend. As regards gross semantic classification, the compound is likely to refer to an insect: s a c a - g ü e y o s 'dragonfly' (= c a b a l l u d e l d i a n t r u, cf. Sp. folksy caballito del diablo beside learned libélula), s a l t a - p r a o s 'grasshopper' (= Sp. salta-montes); or to a small bird: p i c a - t u e r t o s 'species of bird nibbling at blossoms and fruit'; or to a plant: p a t a - l l o b u 'kind of large-sized clover' (lit. 'wolf's paw'). However, the frame of reference may be entirely different, either facetious: m o x a c á n 'cutaneous

---

[21]Cf. C. P. Otero's latest review article in Romance Philology, XXI (1967-68), 42-66, esp. 55-59, with references to two earlier publications of my own.

infection,' 'ill-mannered ('rough-surfaced'?) child or adult' (lit. 'spot sullied
by dog's urine' = b o t - a d a); also c a b u - m u n d u 'lamb's caecum' (lit.
'end of the world'; speaking of a hog's intestines one uses x u a n instead);
or strictly matter-of-fact: c u e r d a - c a r r u 'thick, strong rope, used to
tie the load to the wagon,' lit. 'wagon-rope'; m a n - c u s p i u 'spittle used to
moisten the hands in grasping a tool.' The syntactic relation of the two ingredients may be that of qualifier vs. noun, a schema hardly characteristic
of truly vernacular preferences (one culturally noteworthy relic of the older
use of <u>sexta</u>-<u>feria</u> 'Friday,' familiar from Portuguese, is the stereotyped
phrase f a c é s e s t a - f e r i a = s e s t a - f e r i - a r 'to repair roads and
paths, to prune, pave, and clean up, to engage in chores normally reserved
for Fridays'[22]). More characteristic of folk-speech is the lapidary juxtaposition of verb and noun; the verb appears in its barest form, outwardly
resembling the imperative in its severe economy of size, while the noun in
post-position may be the subject of the verb (m e x a - c á n), or its direct
object; cf. supra p i c a - t u e r t o s, s a c a - g ü e y o s; add obviously modern
c i e r r a - p o l l e r u 'zip' (= Sp. <u>cierre</u>-<u>relámpago</u>),[23] or a localizer of the
action (cf. s a l t a - p r a o s, supra). Where two nouns are juxtaposed the
second may play the part of the qualifier or the possessor, as in p a t a -
l l o b u 'wolf's paw,' c a b u - m u n d u lit. 'world's end,' c u e r d a - c a r r u
'rope for the wagon.' If the noun precedes the verb, it will have the flavor of
a loosely attached object, thus: m a n - 'with or on the hand'; hence m a n -
c o r n - i - a r 'to bump, bruise oneself' (Rato y Hevia: 'to hurt one's hand,'
cf. Sp. <u>corn</u>-<u>ear</u> 'to butt, horn') and the aforementioned m a n - c u s p - i u.

   Under favorable circumstances there may develop a border zone between
composition and affixation. Thus, a word like u ñ a 'nail, claw' is imagerially
far too exciting not to tease the speakers' imagination, and its presence is
likely to be felt behind such verbs as a - p a l p - u ñ - a r 'to rumple, handle
roughly,' almost 'to crush,' m a s - u ñ - a r 'to finger,' etc.; cf. Section 211 (i),
infra. (D. Catalán, alternatively, prefers to start out from <u>apuñar</u>.) On the
other hand, - u ñ - a r fits quite snugly into the purely suffixal series ("vocalic gamut") dominated by - a ñ - a r and - i ñ - a r, cf. p i z c - a ñ - a r 'to
pinch.'[24] In this instance it is conceivably permissible to speak of semi-
compounds.

[22] The limitation of this word to a single set phrase entitles us to declare it a relic,
even in descriptive analysis.

[23] One is here reminded of <u>poll</u>-<u>era</u>, which is used in some varieties of Spanish
(for instance, in Argentinian) for <u>falda</u> 'skirt.'

[24] It thus becomes necessary to separate (a) - u ñ u, the genuine adjectival suffix
attached to zoonyms (= Sp. -<u>uno</u>; cf. Ast. c e r b - u n u 'wild'), and the derivatives
branching off from such adjectives (e.g., p e r r - u ñ u = e m - p e r r - u ñ - a u 'stubborn,

Another area of transition between composition and affixal derivation is the coinage of derivatives from compounds. Thus, from p a p - a l b a , lit. 'white dewlap or double chin,' specifically applying to the hog, speakers have extracted the diminutive p a p - a l b - i n a , using it as a substitute for the original designation (threatened by taboo) of the 'weasel.' There is no record of the local use of *a l b i n u as a free form. Slightly different, it would seen, is the status of p i c u - c e r b - a l , one of at least three local names of the 'woodpecker.' One is left wondering whether any peculiarity of stress or juncture has prevented Canellada from transcribing this label in two words, p i c u   c e r b a l , the latter a derivative from (one gathers) c i e r b u 'stag' —a coinage made necessary by the deviant semantic content of c e r b - u n u 'wild, rebellious, intractable.'

130. Relation of gender to suffixal derivation.

As usually happens in Romance dialectology, certain crucial facets of the relationship between gender and suffixation in the Cabranes dialect defy easy and accurate classification. The three worst offenders are (a) the post-verbal nouns; (b) a strong minority of diminutives, augmentatives, and the like which happen to diverge in gender from the underlying primitives; (c) masculine and feminine "doublets"—some involving primitives, others suffixal derivatives—with varying degrees of semantic differentiation.

131. The gender of postverbal nouns.

Like other varieties of Romance—though perhaps on a more modest scale than the average—the lexicon of our dialect includes a masculine and a feminine series of such nouns, clearly set off by certain formal features (the endings - u and - a , respectively, plus stress on the stem), as match semantically corresponding verbs, typically in - a r .[25] It will be recalled that the exact hierarchy of noun and verb has here been neutralized (see Section 110, supra). The formula behind the distribution of - u and - a variants, in either synchronic or diachronic view, seems very elusive. Thus,

---

obstinate,' cf. Sp. e m - p e r r - a d o 'doggish') from (b) - u ñ u (noun) and - u ñ - a r (verb) in c a b r - u ñ u 'edge of a scythe,' c a b r - u ñ - a r 'to hone a scythe' (which both give at first the erroneous impression of similarly flanking c a b r a 'goat'), and both, in turn, (c) from such verbs in - u ñ - a r (as well as from their offshoots) as betray the influence of u ñ a 'nail, claw,' thus approaching the status of compounds.

[25]One finds hardly any trace of masculine postverbals in - e ; referring as it does to a wind, l l e b a n t e , contrary to Canellada's assertion, is clearly not a case in point, cf. n. 8, supra. But note d e s - i g ü - e (beside - a) 'disorder, disarrangement,' flanking d e s - i g u - a r 'to disarrange,' and d e s - l l e c h - e 'weaning,' flanking d e s - l l e c h - a r = d e s - a - t e t - a r .

the two relevant offshoots from r o z - a r 'to grub, stub, clear (land)':
r o z - u '(under)brush' and r o z - a 'enclosed land, rich in shrubbery and
other plant growth' (= ll e n d - ó n 'pasture ground'), are minimally distinguished on the semantic side, while r o z - a d a 'cleared terrain' stands
apart quite neatly; f i l - a 'spinning' (beside f i l - a r 'to spin,' 'to form an
even, gentle flow' [speaking of oil]) and f i s g - a 'crack, split' beside f i s g -
a r (= r e s g - a r) 'to rip, tear open' have been preferred to counterparts
in - u for no apparent grammatical reason. There may, on closer inspection, emerge a lexical reason in such an impasse: The place of f i l u has
been preempted by the well-entrenched word for 'thread'—which, language
historians assure us, sequentially even preceded f i l - a r .[26] On the synchronic plane it may be argued that, with certain key-verbs, the post-verbals
—suggestive of the action itself as well as of its results and its locale—are
often allowed to occupy in the structure a niche that has been left empty, and
that on the model of important relationships so defined (say, f i l - a : - a r)
speakers are apt at any moment to produce new words similar in imagerial
content (synonymy, antonymy, metaphors) and in the distribution of dominant
formal features (number of syllables, word-initial consonant, nuclear vowel,
etc.); hence f i s g - a : - a r .

132. Discrepancy in gender between primitive and derivative.

Where modifying suffixes—mostly confined to emotional orchestration—
are pressed into service, one expects in Hispano-Romance, in marked contrast to Italian,[27] change of gender only on a severely limited scale. This
expectation is ordinarily fulfilled in Cabranes, witness f o n t - a s c - a ,
- a s q u - i n a 'small spring, puddle fed and emptied by running water'—presumably subordinated to f u e n t e ; f a b - a r - a c a 'dry and seedless bean-
pod' beside f a b a '(kidney-)bean' (= Sp. hab-ich-uela, judía); but then one
finds also f o n t - á n 'stream, rivulet,' f o n t - a s c - u (tagged as a synonym
of - a s c a), and f o n t - a y u 'small spring, thinly flowing source.' To revert
to the family of '(kidney-)bean,' one observes the contrast between f a b - o n a
'broad bean' (= Sp. haba de mayo) and f a b - u c u 'small-sized broad bean.'

[26] Actually FĪLĀRE is a Late Latin replacement (extracted from FĪLUM 'thread')
for classical NĒRE; see A. Ernout and A. Meillet, Dictionnaire étymologique de la
langue latine, 4th ed. (Paris, 1959-60), p. 235a.

[27] The grammaticized usage of Italian shines through in such (obligatory) relationships as cas-a 'house' : -ino 'small house'; tavol-a 'table' : -ino 'small table'; donn-a
'woman' : -one (m.) 'stout, robust woman, virago.' Within the ranks of diminutives,
the masculine may act as a lame substitute for the I-E neuter; cf. G. -chen, -lein;
Russ. dom-iško (m., but with a neuter ending) 'small, miserable house' alongside
dom (m.).

Assuming f l o r 'flower' is feminine on the local scene, as is generally true
in Hispano-Romance, the gender and ending of f l o r - i t u (or - i - a t u)
'field flower, ordinary flower' are conspicuous. One is here reminded of Sp.
cas-uco 'shack, shanty' beside casa 'house,' or of ventan-illo, -ico 'peep-
hole' and -uc(h)o 'ugly little window' beside ventana 'window,' or else of
vill-orr-io 'small country town' beside villa 'town,' which coexist peacefully
with cas-illa 'cabin, booth, post-office box,' ventan-illa 'small window,
wicket,' and vill-or-ía 'hamlet, farm,' all three completely lacking in overtones of contempt and commiseration. In both the standard and the Cabranes
dialect, then, change of gender under comparable circumstances carries with
it, by way of separate dimension, a distinctly stronger value judgment. On
this string of problems see Erica C. García's forthcoming article in Romance
Philology: "Gender Switch in Romance Derivation."

 133. Masculine and feminine doublets.

These difficulties are compounded when one relates, not the derivative
to the primitive, but sets of two (or more) words of comparable rank, whether
primitives or derivatives. In the ranks of animal names, one would expect,
in any parallel arrangement, the masculine form, as a matter of course, to
denote the male and its exact feminine equivalent the female of the species;
but even this trivial prediction does not invariably come true. The foreseeable distribution may apply to l l o n d - u ~ - a 'otter,' where the feminine
provides the generic name (vars.: l l ó n - d r i a , - d r i g a , - t r i a ,
- t r i g a); also, among phytonyms, to f e l e c h - u 'male fern' beside - a
'female fern.' But c u e r b - u designates the 'raven,' apparently regardless
of sex, whereas c u e r b - a is the label for a smaller and blacker bird (=
c h o b a); in derivatives such as c u e r b - e r - í a 'large flock of . . . ; the
din produced by such a flock,' the dividing-line between c u e r b - u and - a
is inevitably blurred. Similarly, l l a n g o s t - a refers to the 'bumblebee
appearing by St. John's day,' - u (or -í n) to 'any insect resembling a
coleopteran'; l l o b - u 'wolf' is flanked by - a 'mole cricket.' Perhaps one
can place here f o r m i g - a 'ant' (its existence, though unauthenticated, is
above suspicion) vs. f o r m i g - o s 'kind of meal involving grated bread,
eggs, and honey' (appreciated as a tidbit)—do the crumbs of grated bread
recall a procession of ants?
 In the sharply delimited domain of tools and containers there is no lack
of feminines denoting the larger piece or the larger set—the classic pattern
of distribution, e.g., c a c í - u 'any ordinary receptacle' vs. - a 'ensemble
of such vessels'; similarly, a b l a n u refers to a 'small hard elongated
hazelnut,' b e n t - á n (also - a n u) to a 'small, unimportant, oddly placed
window,' t o r t u to a 'smaller-than-usual cake' (as against a b l a n a ,

t o r t a , and—conjecturable—b e n t a n a identifying the standard objects).
But these clear-cut instances, discernibly, represent a minority, albeit a
sizable one; there are other cases where the masculine and the feminine
are (inaccurately?) defined as exact synonyms: f o r n - i e l l u / - i e l l a
'pile of brushwood or rubbish burned in a meadow,' m u r - i - u / - i - a 'wall,'
r e s t - i e l l - u / - a 'carding board studded with iron prongs,' and many
others where the principal difference between the two items contrasted is
not one of size, but rather one of make, shape, and purpose (the unequal
size may, of course, remain a concomitant), or where these simply cannot
be paired off despite an overlap of semantic substance. Thus   d u e r n - a
is a 'wooden vessel or trough' (used to catch the cider dripping from the
apple press, or to knead the dough for cake, or to dress a slaughtered hog),
while   d u e r n - u is a 'wooden rack or manger used in feeding hogs.'
F o r c - a (implied by f o r c - a u 'bifurcated,' etc.) is the familiar 'pitchfork'; the innovatory f o r c - u measures the spaces between the outstretched
thumb and index finger; f o r n - u 'furnace, stove' (securely hypothesized)
clashes with f o r n - a 'oven (separated from the kitchen) for baking bread';
f o r n - i c - u 'cavity in the wall, next to the kitchen, for storing ashes needed
in bleaching' contrasts with - i c - a (f u e n t e   d e   . . .) 'stream covered
by a layer of stones or of gypsum.' Examine further f u s - u 'spindle,' as
against f u s - a 'thread wrapped around the spindle' (cf. f u s - a u 'spindleful'
= Sp. hus-ada); l l u e z - u 'hollow (walnut, hazelnut), rotten (egg), cracked
(bell)' vs. l l u e z - a (adj.) 'brooding,' speaking of hens; (noun) 'treacherous
swampy ground that engulfs the unwary' (= l l a m a r g a) —the frame of comparison here is acoustic, not graphic;[28] m a y - u 'wooden hammer for pulping
apples' vs. m a y - a 'tamper for crushing clods'; m u e r g - u 'bitter hull sur-
rounding the walnut' vs. m u e r g - a 'black dye (= c o r t i e g a) exuded by
that hull.'

In view of this extraordinary multiplicity of relationships—hardly any two
pairs chosen at random appear identically structured—it may seem necessary
to revise, in the direction of enhanced liberalization, several existing hypo-
theses on the augmentative feminine and, paradoxically enough, on its opposite, the feminine diminutive. Thus, toward the conclusion of their weighty
inquiry into these phenomena Henry and Renée Kahane declared twenty years
ago: "The masculine ~ feminine contrast is used to indicate either that the
feminine is larger than the masculine, or that the feminine is smaller" (p.

[28] On the ill-definable relationship of clueca to llueza see Wagner's article (supra,
n. 1), pp. 374f.

173).[29] Without denying the existence of these two sharply contoured kernels one is free to surmise that masculines have been and are being extracted from feminines, and vice versa, in dialects such as the one under investigation with relatively little concern about the sizes of the objects involved. The mechanism of derivation in many instances provides a simple means for coining a new word referentially related to the old word, where it would have been cumbersome, overnice, or otherwise inadvisable to use a more precise suffix for the neatest possible identification of the relationship. Putting it colloquially, this is, by Romance standards, the easy, the lazy way of deriving a new word.

[29]"The Augmentative Feminine in the Romance Languages," Romance Philology, II (1948-49), 135-175. For the latest major appraisal of a spate of studies bearing on this problem (including a few by B. Hasselrot) see J. R. Craddock's splendid "Critique . . . " referred to in n. 10, supra.

Part Two

AN ANALYTICAL INVENTORY OF
DERIVATIONAL SUFFIXES

210. Preliminary considerations.

There may attach, as I indicated at the outset, a certain advantage to segregating all those suffixes that enter into groups presided over by vocalic gamuts from those that do not lend themselves to such classification. The existing literature on word-formation has for decades, sporadically and incidentally, alluded to these gamuts, but one sorely misses any attempt to treat the phenomenon on a monographic scale, and such inventories of Hispano-Romance derivational suffixes as one encounters at rare intervals, fail to use these gamuts as a major taxonomic device. The main benefit that may some day accrue to linguists from this alternative approach to morphemic classification will in all likelihood affect historically-slanted studies, since perfect prototypes available in the parent language (-$\bar{A}G\bar{O}$, -$\bar{I}G\bar{O}$, -$\bar{U}G\bar{O}$; -$\bar{A}MEN$, -$\bar{I}MEN$, -$\bar{U}MEN$, etc.) raise the question of proliferation; but it seems, for obvious reasons, methodologically sounder to start the experiment with a few tentative descriptive analyses.

Vocalic gamuts may include—in Asturian no less than in cognate dialects —as many as five members each, as is familiar from parallel situations in standard Spanish (-arro, -orro/-urro; -azo, -izo, -uzo; -án, -ín, -ón; -ajo, -ejo, -ijo, -ujo; etc.), and the vowels at the present evolutionary stage may either be monophthongs or may represent peaks of rising diphthongs; cf. Ast. -agu, -iegu, -ugu; Sp. dial. -aco, -ieco, -ueco. (The emergence of the diphthongs, traceable to open vowels, goes back to a less than very remote past, so that one easily visualizes a stage at which the gamuts were all entirely governed by interplays of richly nuanced monophthongs.)

The familiar experience that stressed front vowels are more tidily distinguished than stressed back vowels repeats itself at this point: While -eco and -ico, -ejo and -ijo, -ete (dial. also -eto) and -ito convey sharply differentiated messages, it is practically impossible to draw any comparably neat dividing line between -orro and -urro or -oño, -ueño, and -uño.[30]

---

[30]On the other hand, interfixes (pretonic by definition), -ech- and -ich-, -eg- and -ig-, -err- and -irr-, to cite just three pairs, are found in almost free variation, and fluctuation sometimes engulfs a variants as well (e.g., -ag-); for illustrations see my article "Studies in the Hispanic Infix -eg-," Language, XXV (1949), 139-181.

This observation applies alike to standard Spanish and to the majority of dialects.

At this juncture it must be stressed that the characteristic Hispano-Romance derivational suffix, whether or not it happens to fit into a gamut, begins with a stressed vowel or with a semiconsonant immediately preceding such a vowel; cf. Ast. -achu, -ada beside -au, -al/-ar, -eño and -iño, on the one hand, and, on the other, among the more isolated items, -ez(a), -ía, -or/-ura, also -i(e)llu, -ientu, and -uelo. Where the affix, after the subtraction of the radical, turns out to contain at least one syllable preceding the one marked by the stressed vowel, we usually face a combination ("chain") of interfix and genuine suffix. In most instances it is possible to arrange the pretonic vowels of interfixes into separate gamuts, but the problems this array poses are slightly different from those raised by authentic suffixes (cf. Section 115, supra). It is interesting, for example, after discovering -iquín /ikin/, an obvious "chain," to ask oneself whether /ik/ similarly precedes /an/ and /on/ or whether /ak/ and /uk/ are tolerated before /in/—a legitimate question of morphotactics involving the juxtaposition of two derivational suffixes, of which the first, in this context, has been demoted to the humbler role of an interfix.[31] In other cases falling under this rubric, however, the concatenator or interfix pressed into service is the fragment of an inflectional morpheme (past-participial, gerundial, etc.), with the result that the choice of the allomorph is primarily controlled by the respective conjugational class: cf., in the Cabranes material, -ad- and -ed- before -era, -and- before -era, -ad- and -id- before -or(a) and before -ura.[32] We are here almost at the opposite pole from the gamuts of stressed vowels, which—whatever their ultimate origins in proto-Latin—have, at the Romance stage, achieved almost total independence from the three or four conjugation classes of each dialect. Also, the

[31]Mant-(iqu)-ín 'lover, boy-friend' and prob-iqu-ín, from probe 'poor, wretched,' which is metathesized pobre (pp. 13 and 260). Similarly may-uelu 'big boy' (lit. 'clapper of bell') beside may-uel-ón 'boy who has [rapidly] grown a good deal,' 'strikingly tall fellow.'

[32]Cf. llab-ad-era 'laundry' (abstr.) = Sp. lavado 'the issue of washing'; com-ed-era 'food' (abstr.), 'the matter of eating'; llab-and-era (a) 'rock at which the washing is done,' (b) 'wagtail' (= llend-ad-ora, -ar-ina); a-son-sañ-ad-or 'wag, joker, jester, mimic' from a-son-sañ-ar 'to scoff at, make fun of, mimic'; llim-id-or 'expert in knocking down fruit with a pole,' from llim-ir 'to knock down fruits from a tree' (= Sp. varear); clis-ad-ura 'bafflement, astonishment' (lit. 'glare, dazzle'), from clis-ar los güeyos 'to stare' (in the broad domain of 'eclipse'); manc-ad-ura 'injury, sore, gall,' from manc-ar 'to wound.'

interfixes seem less tightly organized; though -er-, as in -(d)er-ía and -er-ina, also -ar-, in almost any context, are both plentifully represented on the local scene, they seem to defy any attempt at meaningful contrast.[33]

Highly atypical, by virtue of their structure, of the rank and file of Hispanic derivational suffixes are adverbial -mente (this is the form actually favored in Cabranes: ¡guapamente que sí! 'I should say so!') and the vehicle of abstracts and mass-nouns, Sp. -miento, Ast. -mientu: a-trist-ay-a-mientu 'entristecimiento,' i.e., 'saddening, depression,' dis-curr-i-mientu 'idea, intuition,' inasmuch as tradition, etymological considerations, and even elements of structural thinking combine to bar the segmentation of -amente into *-am-ente, of -amientu into *-am-ientu and of -imientu into *-im-ientu.[34] We must consequently abide by the conventional breakdown -a-mente, -a-mientu, -i-mientu; as a result, we are saddled with two aberrant derivational suffixes beginning with a consonant ushered in by an extra-brief vocalic link or concatenator. The second considerations apply to -dá (= Sp. -dad), whose link to the preceding segment of the word—not always diaphanous—may even be zero: señal- or señar-dá 'pain, nostalgia, melancholy recollection.'

211. Nominal suffixes entering into vocalic gamuts.

It seems advisable to organize the material, at first, in alphabetical order (i.e., in random fashion), using the consonant pillars or anchors as prime classifiers and the various stressed vowels immediately preceding them as secondary classifiers, and only then, in a separate operation, to search for

---

[33]Cuerb-ería 'flock of ravens, or of somewhat smaller and blacker birds,' 'noise made by such a flock'; bey-ur-d-er-ía '(ugly old woman's) grimace,' in the last analysis from bieyu 'old,' cf. b(i)ey-era 'old age' (= It. vecchi-aia), an elaboration on bey-ures (pl.) 'grimaces,' bey-ur-eru 'grimacing,' with a measure of collateral support from belord-ería 'trifle, useless and pointless thing,' which calls to mind Fr. ba-lourd-ise 'gross blunder, doltishness.' The counterparts include dulc-er-ina 'small, sweet cherry,' llech-er-ina 'yellow-blossomed plant, thriving amid grass, with a milky sap.'

[34]The Hispano-Romance adverbs are at the mid-point between composition and derivation, as can be demonstrated syntactically. As regards -mientu, its Latin ancestor in certain cases needed no vocalic link to the radical (FRAGMENTUM, FIGMENTUM), whence the Latinist's justification for carving out -MENTUM. The close ties, in Spanish, between -mento (including cases like learned frag-mento, seg-mento), -menta (vesti-menta 'clothes'), -miento, and -mienta (herra-mienta 'set of tools') is one potent reason for our refusal to operate with -(i)ento; another is the separate existence of the semantically irreconcilable adj. -(i)ento, cf. Sp. mugr-iento 'dirty,' viol-ento 'impetuous, short-tempered.'

any emergent patterns as regards both the consonants and the vowels involved in this interplay. We shall examine separately the nominal and the verbal elements.

(a) The C̲ /k/ pillar

(α) - a c u , with a wide range of overtones (including, as a rule, the suggestion of 'crudeness, coarseness'): b e r r - a c u 'ill-tempered man' (lit. 'wild boar [foaming at the mouth],' surrounded by congeners, cf. Section 111, supra); f a b - a r - a c a 'pod of the (kidney-)bean (f a b a), dry and seedless; idle talk'; m e ñ - a c a beside m e ñ a 'doll, toy,' reminiscent of Sp. muñ-eca 'doll' and, in other respects, of Ptg. men-ina 'girl'; similarly g o c h - a c u beside g o c h u 'hog'; p i t - a c u beside p i t - u 'young chick,' - ó n 'rooster,' - e r u 'hen-coop'; r a p a z - a c u beside r a p a z u 'lad' (p. 28). This element enters into the many-pronged family f u r - a c u 'hole,' - a c a 'opening in a hedge,' - a q u - e r a 'something full of needles,' - a x - a c a 'small hole,' all flanking f u r - a r 'to bore' (cf. Ptg. bur-aco 'hole'); otherwise its affinity to names of living beings is sharply pronounced.

(β) - i c u , suffixal in f o l l - i c u 'sth. hollow and empty like a pair of bellows' (f u e l l e , recorded in a special sense in the context of a prank), also in f o r n - i c u 'hollow space in the wall, near the kitchen, for the storage of ashes,' - i c a 'spring covered with a layer of stone and gypsum,' beside f o r n a 'oven,' cf. further g u a r - i c a 'cowardly man' (reminiscent of Sp. mar-ica 'sissy, milksop,' -ic-ón 'homosexual')—conceivably related to g u a r - (i) - a r 'to incubate,' which one is tempted to relate to Sp. hue-, güe-ro 'addle' (adj.). As an interfix - i c u enters into - i q u - í n (cf. Section 115, supra; add c a r r - i q u - í n de dios [or del r e y] 'Ursa'); and as a suffixoid it functions in f o c - i c u 'snout, face' (= Sp. hoc-ico), esp. in the phrase p o n e r   f o c i c u (= e n - f o c - i c - á - s e) 'to grow angry.' It suggests melioratively 'smallness,' blended with 'exquisiteness'; pejoratively, 'effeteness, emptiness, futility.'

(γ) - u c u , clearly detachable in f a b - u c u 'small-sized broad bean' (f a b - a), m a y - u c a 'peeled and dried chestnut' beside m a y a 'tamper used to pound clods'; cf. the homonymous suffixoid in W.-Ast. mer-uca (Acevedo and Fernández), Cabranes - u c u 'earthworm,' which Lausberg traces to BRUCHUS with a qualifying query answered by our analysis. The central idea seems to be 'smallness' devoid of 'exquisiteness.'

(b) The CH /č/ pillar

(α) -achu: c e n - a c h u, used in near-by communities (= Cabranes p a x u), 'basket made from unpolished sticks, shaped like a half-sphere and used for freshly cut grass.' Not neatly detachable and, as a result, semantically hazy.

(β) -ichu: entering, as an interfix, into playfully diminutive p i q u - i r r - i c h - í n 'tiny,' snugly matching W.-Ast. pequ-irr-ich-ín (Acevedo and Fernández), from pequ- 'small' arrived at through subtraction of -eño.[35]

(c) The D-pillar

Here the local situation is radically different from the state of affairs in Spanish. Whereas the standard language offers the four sharply delineated sub-clusters of suffixes (α) -ada, -ida (orig. action nouns of past-participial background, later mass-nouns, etc.) (β) -ado, -ido (action nouns, later designations of rank, etc.), (γ) -ado, -ido, -udo (adjectives with overtones of resemblance, scarcity, and overabundance, respectively), (δ) -edo, -eda (mass-nouns, indicative particularly of plantations), an accident of local sound-development has completely segregated in Cabranes - a d a from - a u < - a d o, - e u < - i d o, and - i u < - i d o, while preserving the pillar of - u d u intact. The - d -, in other words, has survived only where its loss would have entailed (unstable) sequences of identical vowels, such as * - a a and * - u u. A further complication arises from the divergent treatment of d before stressed i and before /j/, a discrepancy accounting for the coexistence of - a d i e g u and - a í z u (= Sp. -adizo). One can thus, by way of exception, speak, at most, of stray remnants of the original D pillar:[36]

---

[35]Cf. Sp. ri-ach-uelo 'rivulet,' in a recoil from phonotactically unattractive *ri-uelo; the vowel sequence it displays contrasts with that of hab-ich-uela 'kidney-bean, string bean' (from haba). Rather characteristically, - a c h (u) and - i c h (u) function in Hispano-Romance more frequently as elusive suffixoids and interfixes (alternating in this latter role with - a n c h - and - e n c h - / (- i n c h -) than as straight suffixes. For a few shreds of preliminary information see my article "The Two Sources of the Hispanic Suffix -azo, -aço," Language, XXXV (1959), 193-258, esp. 215-224.

[36]The range of - a u can be exemplified with d u e r n - a u 'the contents of a wooden vessel, used to catch the cider flowing from the press, etc.' (d u e r n - a, - u), f o r c - a u 'front prop of a wagon,' (adj.) 'split, cleft,' beside f o r c - a, - ó n, etc.; f u s - a u 'spindleful' beside f u s u 'spindle'; and t r a m - a u 'weft or woof,' 'prepared things,' cf. Sp. trama 'id.' F a y - e u 'beech grove' matches Sp. ha-edo. One kind of apple is called m a z a n a d e c a s t a ñ - e u (Canellada, p. 264); cf. Sp. castañ-eda

(α) -ada: One discovers the expected profusion of meanings characterized by wide semantic dispersal, including:

(αα) 'blow' (for the most part depicted facetiously, owing to such
circumstances as an unusual frame of comparison, an unexpected part
of the opponent's anatomy aimed at, a bizarre tool chosen for delivery
of the blow, etc.): cib(i)ell-ada 'blow with a rope or braid made of
osier' (cib-iella, or, if thicker, -iellu), madreñ-ada 'blow
administered with a wooden shoe,' teller-ada 'blow dealt with the
hand at someone's face' (cf. tellera 'salt pork, carved from close
to the jawbone');

(ββ) 'gesture, rapid movement': cigoñ-, cigüeñ-ada 'wink'
(cf. Sp. guiño, through folk-etymological identification with cigüeña 'stork'),
güey-ada 'glance, wink' (güeyu 'eye,' fig. 'hole in the millstone'),
maza-cu-ada 'blow on the back or side, from a fall' beside maza-
cu-ar 'to fall down,' presumably involving the counterpart of Sp. culo
'buttocks' (D. Catalán reminds me of Sp. culada 'bumps-a-daisy' and of
dar un masculillo 'golpear suavemente el culo contra el suelo a un niño
suspendido por los brazos y los pies');

(γγ) 'amount, quantity': fil-andr-ada 'series of objects strung on
a thread' (cf. Sp. hil-and-ero 'spinner, spinning shop'), fori-at-ada
'soft deposit' beside foria(ta) 'clay, soft excrements,' gay-ada
'pitchforkful of brush or grass' (from gay-ón 'trident, pitchfork'),
golf-ar-ada 'big swallow, puff,' 'big wave, surge' (beside a counter-

---

'chestnut grove' (widespread in onomastics) beside castañ-o 'chestnut tree.' Examples
of -íu matching Sp. -ido and indicative of 'lack, default, inadequacy' include asombríu₁ 'turned pale through constant lack of exposure to the sun' (cf. sombra 'shade'),
conden-íu 'condemned, damned' (as against Sp. condenado), and ¡conxur-íu ~
au! 'id.' (profanity, to curse a child who has done some mischief). On this little-known
use of -i(d)o see my earlier studies in Language, XXII (1946), 302-309, and in Current
Trends in Linguistics, III (1966), 333-336. Locally, the masculine form of this secondary
adjectival -íu has coincided with the older substantival -íu indicative either of a
place (in which case it clearly reflects Lat. -ĪUU; cf. Language, XVII [1941], 99-118;
Modern Language Quarterly, III [1942], 621-646; and Classica et Medievalia, V [1943],
238-256): asombr-íu₂ 'place secluded from the sun'; or of a rhythmically repeated
movement (say, vibration) or sound (say, animal cry), as in onomatopoeically orches-
trated cacar-ex-íu beside -u 'cackling' (flanking the verb cacar-exar = Sp.
cacar-ear), miagu-íu 'meowing' (= Sp. maull-ido), also in cimbl-íu 'vibration'
accompanying the verb cimbl-ar. The last-mentioned derivational model has many
counterparts in Romance, esp. in Italian (mormor-io 'murmur,' etc.); the animal cries
match Sp. -ío and, even more snugly, -ido; cf. E. S. Georges and J. R. Craddock's
trail-blazing article in Romance Philology, XVII (1963-64), 87-107.

part of Sp. golfo 'open sea, main'?)—with these derivatives one is tempted
to class fond-(ig-)on-ada, fond-ig-ay-ada 'lowland, bottom
land,' lit. 'that which fills a depression' (cf. Sp. hond-on-ada beside hond-
ón 'bottom, lowland'); maz-ada 'residue left after the milk has been
churned and the butter has been removed from a special black-clayed,
two-handled pot' (bot-iya).

(δδ) 'various tools': ferr-ada '(iron) bucket' (Sp. herr-ada),
forc-ada 'bifurcated stick made from a branch,' gui(y)-ada 'long
stick with a prick attached to it, used to prod cattle'—all three of transparent background. To this group speakers have also assigned, after a
minor self-explanatory adjustment, meta-(d)a or mitada 'half';
cf. Sp. mitad.

(β) -udu: fegad-udu 'hard soil that resists ploughing' beside
fégadu 'liver' (resistant to the knife?), felech-udu 'abounding in fern
growth or similar to the fern' (felechu), forc-ej-udu 'husky, robust'
(an adaptation of Sp. forc-ej-udo, influenced by the verb forc-ej-[e]ar 'to
struggle, contend'?), miembr-udu 'burly, husky,' with the diphthong
carried over from miembru into the pretonic syllable, as against Sp.
membr-udo.

(d) The G-pillar

There emerges no clear-cut pattern, either grammatically (-agu and
-ugu are typically substantival, -iegu primarily adjectival) or semantically, except for the predominant reference to wildlife (plants, animals) and
humans:

(α) -agu: llim-i-agu 'slug,' cf. (for the stem) Sp. lim-aza and (for
stem and suffix) W.-Ast. llim-aco (Acevedo and Fernández), It. lum-aca;

(β) -iegu, -iega: one of the most characteristic suffixes of Asturian,
mainly attached to the past participle in a way reminiscent of Sp. -ad-ero
and -ad-izo, cf. allab-anc-iegu 'worthy of praise,' ant-ox-ad-iegu
'fickle, whimsical' (from ant-ox-ar, a transparent Castilianism in view
of local güeyu 'eye'), a-pieg-ad-iegu 'contagious,' a-top-ad-iegu
'comfortable, pleasurable'; also found in bi-functional derivatives from
place-names: llaban-, lleban-iegu 'relating to, inhabitant of, Liébana,'
and in miscellaneous adjectives, occasionally substantivized: man-iega
'large basket, without handles,' -iegu 'smaller basket, with handles' (both

from m a n u 'hand'), etc.[37] Its supporting role as a suffixoid is illustrated with f a n - i e g a as against Sp. fan-ega (= 1.58 bushels).

(γ) - u g u : b e r d - u g u 'contraption made of green twigs to catch birds,' neatly contrastable with b e r d e . Cf. Sp. verd-ugo 'twig, scourge, executioner' and its offshoots in -ada, -ado, -al, -azo, -ón, and -illo.

(e) The L-pillar

The vocalic gamut in this case is extra-short, since only - a l and - i l rank as fully developed suffixes; - e l and, on a very restricted scale, - o l function as dimly recognizable suffixoids in some varieties of Hispano-Romance and, under favorable circumstances, may enter into loose relation-ships with - a l and - i l ,[38] but, of all dialects, Asturian is perhaps the least hospitable to them. Although -al and -ar in many sections of the country show such close affinity as to be freely interchangeable (quite apart from the fact that in a few western dialects the phonemic contrast between syl-lable-final -l and -r has in general been neutralized), one cannot isolate any R pillar comparable to the L pillar, because *-ir and *-ur are non-existent, and -er and -or, while eking out a marginal existence (as in Sp. alquil-er 'rent' beside alquil-ar 'to rent,' ol-or 'smell' beside ol-er 'to smell'—cf. Cabr. g o l - o r), are quite isolated and semantically incom-patible with -ar.

(α) - a l , aside from producing adjectives from nouns (f e r i - a l 'sea-sonal,' cf. s e s t a - f e r i a 'Friday chore'), serves to extract the name of the plant, in most instances a fruit tree or bush (invariably feminine), from the name of the corresponding vegetable or fruit: a b l a n - a l 'hazel' beside a b l a n a 'hazelnut' (as against Sp. avellan-o beside -a) or, even more fre-quently, to derive the name of a plantation, grove, etc. from that of the plant at issue: Thus, c á d - a b a 'stem of the burned furze still nibbled by grazing cattle,' 'tall, old furze' coexists with c a d a b - a l 'place full of such furze';

[37]Cf. my monograph "The Hispanic Suffix -(i)ego" in University of California Publi-cations in Linguistics (hereafter, UCPL), IV:3 (1951), 111-213, as well as the twenty-odd reviews of varying length and merit which it has provoked. On p. 28 of her intro-ductory sketch Canellada lists several pertinent derivatives which she later omits from her word-list (presumably names of inhabitants): c a b r a l - i e g u, c a b r a n-i e g u, t o r a c - i e g u. On m a n - i e g u, etc. see Krüger's book review (supra, n. 1), p. 272.

[38]See Anita Katz Levy, "Contrastive Development in Hispano-Romance of Borrowed Gallo-Romance Suffixes," Romance Philology, XVIII (1964-65), 399-429; XX (1966-67), 296-320.

fig. 'very lean, skinny person'; c o t o l l a is the name attached to 'furze' before burning, and the place where it grows in abundance is known as a c o t o l l - a l .[39] Where this latter relationship prevails, as in the cases of a r b e y - a l , f a b - a l , and p a t a t - a l vs. a r b e y u 'pea,' f a b a '(kidney-)bean,' and p a t a t a 'potato,' speakers apparently see no need to distinguish between the plant and the vegetable.[40]

Where the radical contains an l, - a r is favored by virtue of an age-old dissimilatory mechanism;[41] the closer, within the structure of the word, that l is to the suffix, the stronger the speakers' inclination to prefer -ar. Hence a b l a n - a l and - a r are tolerated side by side on account of the interjacent n, but t r i p u (or t r i p a ?) c u l - a r —apparently beside c u l u 'buttocks'—is alone admissible ('hog's intestines used in the preparation of black or blood pudding'); cf. also c u l - a r - o n a 'id.'

(β) - i l : Its status in c a d r - i l 'hip' is difficult to judge, as long as it is dubious whether cadera 'id.,' familiar from Spanish, also thrives on the local scene—which alone would make - i l a suffix. For a parallel example of vocalic syncope cf. m a d e r a 'wood, timber' ~ m a d r - e ñ a 'wooden shoe.'

(f) The LL /λ/ pillar

Only with a certain stretch of the imagination can one invoke a vocalic gamut here, since diphthongal - i e l l u , very common, and monophthongal - o l l u , fairly rare, are far from providing a truly satisfactory match. A redeeming quality of the items here paired off is the absence of any complete semantic incompatibility.[42]

[39]Cf. W. E. Geiger, "'Fruit,' 'Fruit Tree,' and 'Grove' in Spanish: A Study in Derivational Patterning," ibid., XX, 176-186.

[40]While in f e r i - a l the i is part of the stem, the i of f e r r - i - a l 'flintstone'; (adj.) 'healthy, vigorous, robust, thriving' (said of humans, of wheat, etc.) is clearly intercalary. Judging from f e r r - a x e 'set of six nails,' f e r r - e r u 'blacksmith,' f e r r - e r í a 'din, clangor,' f e r r - ó n 'iron axle of a whipping top,' f e r r - u ñ - e n t u (beside f u r r - u ñ - o s u) 'rusty,' the local word for 'iron' must be f i e r r u .

[41]See Knud Togeby's discussion of Rebecca Posner's doctoral thesis ("Qu'est-ce que la dissimilation?," Romance Philology, XVII [1963-64], 642-667) and my own reaction to that controversy, in Language, XLIII (1967), 240-242; also, at greater length, in "Multiple Versus Simple Causation in Linguistic Change," included in the miscellany To Honor Roman Jakobson (The Hague, 1967), II, 1228-47.

[42]In the Cabraniego variety of Central Asturian, palatal l, spelled ll, matches Sp. l- word-initially (l l a b o r = labor, l l a g a r = lagar) and Sp. -ll- word-medially

(α) -iellu is one of the leading diminutive suffixes in the area under survey (for additional comments see Section 214.3). It is attached:

(αα) to clearly identifiable nouns, as in forn-iellu or -iella 'pile of clods torn out with grass (= tapinos) and burned in breaking untilled ground,' lit. 'little stove or oven'; note the contrast between bot-iellu 'stomach' and bot-iya 'black-clayed, two-handled pot with a hole in the bottom, used in churning butter';[43]

(ββ) to miscellaneous nouns no longer clearly silhouetted: far-iellu 'bran,' godob-iellu 'bundle of clothes' (= god-oyu, coll-iñu);

(γγ) to bare verbal stems, esp. if the verb displays an -er or an -ir infinitive: ferb-iella 'benumbment, seizure in breathing; stabbing pain in the chest' beside ferb-er = Sp. herv-ir 'to seethe';

(δδ) to -ar- verbs, with the help of an -ad- linkage: forc-ad-iella 'infection inside a cow's hoof' ("entre las caces"), cf. Sp. pes-ad-illa 'nightmare.'

(β) -ollu is quite exceptional; cf. mig-ollu 'soft part of bread, cake, etc.' alongside miga —conceivably through secondary association with non-decomposable miollu 'marrow, pith' (cf. Sp. meollo, Lat. MEDULLA)—, also pe-g-ollu 'each of the four supports of a small wooden barn or storehouse' (orru), related to the local equivalent of Sp. pie 'foot';[44] to these isolated occurrences add -ollu's role as a suffixoid in gor-ollu 'clot, curd.'

(-iellu = -illo); in special cases C.-Ast. -ll- corresponds to Sp. -ch-; thus sall-ar 'to fall to the ground without ripening' (speaking of fruit), with an action noun in -u and a derivative in -ón 'full-grown, ripe maize,' parallels Sp. sach-ar 'to prune, lop off' < SARCULĀRE (if this relation fails to obtain in the case of sarapullu = sarpull-ido 'rash, eruption,' then the reason for the incongruence is that the latter, an outgrowth of SERPU(S)CULU, is likely to represent a borrowing from Asturo-Leonese, as Corominas persuasively conjectures). At any rate, the Asturian equivalents of Ptg. -alho, Sp. -ajo, etc. are, in the native layer, -ayu and, among adjusted borrowings, -axu; they are discussed farther down, under the Y- and the X-pillars, respectively.

[43]Cf. J. Hubschmid's monograph Schläuche und Fässer (Bern, 1955) and, among its discussions, my review in Language, XXXVIII (1962), 149-185.

[44]Pe-g-ollu reflects plausibly reconstructed *PED-IC-ULLUS; see my paper "A Cluster of Four Homophones in Ibero-Romance," Section 5, in Hispanic Review, XXI (1953), 128-132.

(g) The N pillar

This is easily the most powerful of all consonant pillars, in Asturian even more so than in Castilian on account of the regional distribution of diminutive suffixes, which strengthens it in the North. One can distinguish between a masculine series (-án, -ín, -ón, all three solidly entrenched) and a parallel feminine series, in which -ina and -ona clearly outrank -ana. The symmetry of the design is more sharply pronounced in the singular than in the plural, where -ones and -inos fail to support each other.[45] The feminine series, typically, comprises nouns; the masculine formations hover, in almost unique fashion, between the categories of nouns and adjectives.

(α) -án, quite hazy on the semantic side, may suggest 'affinity, descent, provenience,' e.g., mariñ-án '(ox, cow) known for eating copiously without putting on weight and traceable to the Mariña breed' (hinting at the coastal stretch between Gijón and Tazones); or it may be diminutive: font-án 'small spring'; it matches both Sp. -án and -ano (folg-anz-án 'lazy fellow,' gux-án de seda 'glowworm,' mil-án 'kite').

(β) -ín is diminutive (apart from such isolated cases as trigu-ín 'discernible taste of wheat in bread') and it ordinarily miniaturizes the primitive to which it is attached: balagar-ín 'small conic heap of grass in the meadow,' mant-ín (in affectionate direct address) 'lover boy, honey, sweetheart,' niñ-ín 'baby,' pioy-ín 'small dark bird' (lit. 'little louse'), piquiñ-ín 'little one,' alongside balagar, (a)mante, neñu, pioyu, and, one gathers, pequ-eñu.[46] It also specifies the part of a whole: felech-ín 'growth on the side of a male fern' (felechu, see s.v. -echa). Smallness seems to be subtly implied in the case of gurrumb-ín 'hunchback' beside gurrumbu, also go- and gu-rrumba 'hump' —since a humpbacked person will often appear dwarfish. Occasionally, in particular where the adjectival use prevails, the primitive merely supplies a characterization or qualification, e.g., miguel-inos 'figs—relatively small, yellowish, extra-sweet, and having a stem dotted with white specks —harvested around Michaelmas = San Miguel.'

[45]Cf., in Modern Portuguese, the (etymologically correct) plural endings -ãos (mãos 'hands'), -ães (cães 'dogs'), and -ões (sazões 'seasons'), all three matching singulars in -ão.

[46]Historically, counter to Canellada's belief, pioy-ín is not an onomatopoeia, although it may indisputably have in time acquired secondary onomatopoeic characteristics.

(γ) -ón performs a wide variety of services. In derivatives from nouns, it often functions as a straight augmentative: balagar-ón 'tallest of the conical piles of grass in the meadow,' contrasting diametrically with its semantic opposite -ín (see β, supra); cuyar-ón 'ladle' beside cuyar(a) 'spoon'; fab-ona 'large (kidney-)bean,' alongside faba; forc-ón 'large forklike support' (beside the smaller forc-ada) and, similarly, gay-ón 'strong forked pole'—beside gayu, if such is the local representative of Sp. gajo 'branch of a tree'? In highly facetious derivatives either from verbs or from nouns -ón characterizes a person behaving in a funny, shocking, or reprehensible way. Cf., on the one hand, a-son-sañ-ón 'mimic, clown' beside son-sañ-ar 'to poke fun at, imitate, impersonate,' combay-ón 'flatterer' beside combay-ar 'to flatter, ingratiate oneself,' ferb-oll-ón 'fast, jabbering talker' (ferb-oll-ar 'to seethe'), mas-uñ-ón 'one given to fingering, or one who lets others touch him' beside mas-uñ-ar (= Sp. manosear), me-ón 'one who is always urinating' beside me-ar, tre-bolg-ón 'fast and clumsy talker,' 'one who speaks in spurts or torrents' beside tre-bolg-ar 'to boil, bubble'; and, on the other, madr-eñ-ón 'one who treads too heavily with his wooden shoes (madr-eñes) or walks awkwardly,' manteg-ón 'soft fellow' beside mantega 'butter,' maz-cay-ón 'dolt, simpleton,' an elaboration on mazcayu 'id.' Attached to a noun, -ón may suggest a blow, in rivalry with -ada, -atu, and -azu, cf. calamurn-i-ón 'heavy blow on the head' (cf. Sp. calamorr-ada, -ón, based on [coll.] calamorra 'head') and teller-ón 'blow with one's hand smack in the opponent's face' beside tellera 'hog's bacon, close to his jawbone'; note also fisg-ón, resg-ón 'large rip, shred.' Can one place here clari-ón 'sudden clearing of the sky, between two spells of darkness,' 'bright spot on a poorly-painted wall,' on the assumption that the underlying verb matches Sp. clar-e-ar 'to brighten, dawn, light up, clear up'? Among swift movements one may rank gorfil-ones 'bubbles,' cf. Sp. borbot-ones, though I find no primitive other than the gorg- family to which to attach it. An -ón derivative from a verb less dramatically suggestive of blows may denote a tool, or a place: guind-ón 'wire trap for catching birds' (cf. Sp. guind-ar 'to hoist'), llend-ón 'pasture ground' beside -ar 'to move the cattle about in a meadow,' llimpi-ón 'cleaning mop,' obviously subordinate to -ar (omitted), and taz-ón 'rod used in tilling the soil' beside -ar 'to cut up clods with a special rod' (= facer seches, cortá les seches). Finally, -ón may be the concluding segment of a zoonym, as in mel-ón ~ -andru 'badger.'

The same suffix appears in a number of formations which are on the border line between adjectives and nouns, e.g., fargat-ón 'careless, care-free' (cf. es-fargat-au 'unkempt'), far-iell-ón 'cloying, annoying' beside far-iellu 'bran,' far-iñ-ón (also -osu, -entu) 'floury, soft for work and toil; porridge-fancier' beside far-iña 'flour,' (pl.) -iñes 'porridge,' fart-ón 'voracious eater' beside fart-ar 'to stuff,' felp-ey-ón 'ragged, shabby' beside felp-eyu 'tatter,' and its synonym fes-ori-ón beside fes-oria 'harrow,' foc-ic-ón 'irascible' (cf. the phrase poner foc-icu 'to flare up'), fong-ón (or -osu) 'soft (terrain),' 'fluffy, spongy' (person), no doubt beside fongu 'mushroom' (= Sp. hongo), fori-ón 'suffering from diarrhea (foria), cowardly,' gat-uñ-ón 'one who scratches.'

(δ) -ina refers to a wide variety of small and visibly attractive objects: fruits, berries, vegetables, miscellaneous plants; also nimble, graceful, or flitting animals, birds, etc.: candel-ina, lit. 'little candle' (candela), is a phytonym, alternating with llengua de güé (lit. 'ox-tongue') 'tall plant (shunned by grazing animals), with wide leaves, white blossoms, and a yellow panicle in the center'; cuarent-ina 'small, precociously matur- ing kidney bean, which bears forty (cuarenta) days after it is sown'; dulc-er-ina 'small, very sweet cherry'; llech-er-ina 'yellow- blossomed plant thriving amid grass, shunned by cattle, and exuding a milky sap'; man-ina de Dios 'honeysuckle,' lit. 'God's little sister,' beside mana (in direct, affectionate address) 'sis(ter)'; palomb-ina 'small, white butterfly' beside palomba 'pigeon, dove,' -ar 'dovecote'; pap- alb-ina 'weasel,' lit. 'whitish double chin or lower neck' (propitiatory?); pas-er(-in)a 'short ladder placed outdoors,' etc. Far less commonly, -ina refers to a (liquid or viscous) substance, e.g., cuern-ina 'soft sub- stance concealed inside a horn' (cuernu).

(ε) -ona, in reference to inanimate objects, is a straight augmentative suffix: cul-ar-ona '(thick) intestine leading to the anus.'[47] Applied to humans, -ona marks female agentives: pel-uc-ona 'woman following the plough and picking up the ears,' beside pel-uc-ar 'to pluck flowers, pick up ears.'

---

[47]The by-form cuay-ar-ona 'id.'—if authentic—seems to show a measure of contamination with cuay-ar 'to curdle,' surely the result of a phonetic accident. As shown by maza-cu-ar 'to fall (on one's buttocks),' some forms lacking the nuclear -l- seem to have invaded Cabranes from the West (see Section 211(c), supra, and n. 54, infra); thus *cu(y)-ar-ona—with antihiatic y, as in OSp. des-nuyo 'naked' alongside des-nudo—may have arisen at the fringe of the cul-ar-ona area. The inter- ference of cuay-ar, if confirmed, would then represent a tertiary phase of the process.

(h) The NZ /nθ/ pillar

The maximally neat contrasts would be presented by -ancia and
-encia, -anza and -(i)enza (cf. Section 214.3, infra). What one often
actually finds instead are back-formations ending in -ienzu or marked
by other deviations that tend to break the perfect symmetry:

(α) -ancia (alternating with interfix -anz-): folg-ancia 'loafing'
(= Sp. holg-az-an-ería), folg-a(n)z-án 'loafer,' cf. the phrase de
folgu-eta 'by way of bumming'; allab-anc-iegu 'praiseworthy' (cf.
Sp. alab-anza 'praise').

(β) ferb-ienzu 'hotspell, exposure to scorching sun' beside ferb-er
'to seethe.'[48]

(i) The Ñ /ɲ/ pillar

The word-final segments -añu, -iñu, and -uñu and their feminine
equivalents are all represented in the ranks of the dialect's nouns, as full-
fledged suffixes and as suffixoids alike (with a good deal of fluctuation:
guañu ~ güiña ~ guña 'first shoot of a germinating seed,' with matching verb: gua-, güi-ñar), while -eño is a rare, fossilized adjectival
suffix found in an occasional substantivized formation. As regards -uñu,
it is worth repeating that neither cabr-uñu 'whetting of a scythe; its
sharp cutting edge' nor cabr-uñar 'to hone (a scythe)' are associatively,
still less genetically, connected with cabra 'goat,' though adjectival derivatives in -uño (as a variation upon -uno) from names of domestic animals
are by no means unknown in Hispano-Romance.[49]

(α) -añu, distinctly infrequent, is found, typically, as a suffixoid: argaña 'species of noxious plant,' ber-añu 'summer' (= Sp. ver-ano).

[48]Ast. ferv-ienzu recalls OSp. fe-, fi-m-iença 'fervor, vehemence, religious
zeal,' sim-iença 'seed,' etc., so far as the diphthongization is concerned; see my
papers "Three Spanish-Portuguese Etymologies . . . ," Romanic Review, XXXV
(1944), 307-323, and "The Development of . . . -ANTIA and -ENTIA . . . ," UCPL,
I:4 (1945).

[49]For details see my article "Nuevas aportaciones para el estudio del sufijo -uno,"
Nueva Revista de Filología Hispánica, XIII (1959; publ. in 1960), 241-290. The rather
numerous verbs in -uñar, which, we recall, may be assigned a place midway between derivation proper and composition, e.g., a-palp-uñ-ar 'to touch, grope,
finger' beside (a)palp-ar, (a-r)ra(m)p-uñ-ar 'to snatch, carry away,'
related to the rap- complex, and (a-r)rasc-uñ-ar 'to scratch' (see Section
123, supra), lack nominal counterparts.

(β) -iñu: far-iña 'flour,' (pl.) -iñes 'maize porridge' (= farra-pes); Mar-iña 'name of nearby coastal stretch,' 'livestock (traceable to that breed) owned by one farmer.'

(γ) -eñu: greñu 'curly, disheveled' (speaking of hair), orig. non-suffixal (cf. Sp. greña 'shock of hair'); madr-eña 'wooden shoe,' loosely attached to madera 'wood, timber'; red-eña 'fibrous substance sticking to the hog's intestines' (beside red 'net'?).

(δ) -oñu/-uñu: ferr-uñ-entu 'rusty,' for-oñ(-os-)u 'worm-eaten, mothy' (= a-for-oñ-au, vs. Rato's forr-oñ-osu) beside for-uñu 'dust made by wood-borer' (= Sp. carcoma), ruñu 'dirt adhering to the skin' flanked by ruñ-entu, -osu 'oxydized.'[50]

(j) The RI /rj/ pillar

Since -ar, we recall, cannot be paired off with any other nominal suffix, still less absorbed into a triad,[51] only -ariu, -eriu, and -oriu (or their feminine counterparts) qualify for inclusion in a set; strictly speaking, anchored to the /rj/, not to the bare /r/, pillar. The first, distinctly rare, appears as an ingredient of an occasional distorted Latinism; the second, equally uncommon, figures in llac-eria 'misery, sickness' (cf. OSp. lazeria);[52] the third, highly productive and, as a rule, attached to the past

[50]Historically, -uñ-u/-a reflects -ŪGINE, which locally has cut its ties to -ĀGINE (cf. podr-én 'something that is rotting'; see Language, XIX [1943], 256-258) and -ĪGINE (cf. trigu-ín 'sharp taste of wheat'). This virtual disintegration of a promising vocalic gamut may be attributable to the vigorous rise of a set of diminutive-augmentative suffixes arrogating the right to the same pillar (-ín, -ón, etc.), a schema into which the descendants of -GINE words did not snugly fit. In some varieties of Hispano-Romance -ĀGINE has been superseded by -aña, -eña and -ĪGINE by -iña; also, -ŪGINE > -uña has sporadically received support from PŌTIŌNE 'drink, poison,' OSp. poz-ón, -oña, cf. "Diachronic Hypercharacterization in Romance," Archivum Linguisticum, X (1958), 2-4, with references to older literature. As this monograph is going to press, Jonathan L. Butler's California (Berkeley) dissertation, "The Latin Derivational Suffixes -ĪNUS, -ĪNA, -ĬNUS, and -ĬNEUS: Their Origin and Romance Descendants," just completed, bids fair to overthrow much of our earlier thinking on the -N- pillar.

[51]Gol-or 'smell,' I repeat, may be said to involve an -or derivative from the verb (gol-er?) matching Sp. ol-er 'to smell,' and there exists non-decomposable mug-or 'smell suggestive of dirt and moisture, esp. the stench exuded by unwashed laundry,' a more faithful reflex of MŪCŌRE than is Sp. mugre. But such random traces of -or as suffix and suffixoid (a satellite of -ura) hardly suffice to make it a running mate with -ar (a satellite of -al), given their total semantic irreconcilability.

[52]See my article on lazerar and lazeria in Nueva Revista de Filología Hispánica, VI (1952), 209-276.

participle, enters chiefly into technical rustic words. Functionally, stylistically, and stratigraphically, then, -oriu matches both mock-learned -ariu and its vernacular doublet -eru:

(α) metrin-ariu 'veterinary' (not decomposable).

(β) cobert-oriu 'lid of, or cover for, the kneading trough';[53] col-ad-oriu 'rock—with a groove for running water—on which the vat or tub containing wet, bleached clothing is placed,' beside col-ar 'to strain,' also used for 'strainer' (= Sp. colador); compon-ed-oriu 'leaven, yeast' (= formientu), beside compon-er; facetious com-prend-ed-oriu, or -a 'brains' (cf. coll. Sp. en-tend-ed-eras 'id.'), beside com-prend-er; fes-oria 'hoe, spud' (and, fig., fes-ori-ón 'carelessly dressed' = 'hit with a hoe'?), against the distant background of fis-g-ar 'to rip, tear'; mes-ories 'pair of matched, sharpened sticks, used to harvest wheat,' beside mes-ar 'to tear off or pick with one's bare hands' (grass, hazelnuts, straw, hair). Observe the jocular semantics of coll. Sp. trag-ad-eras 'gullet' > 'naiveté, credulity.'

(k) The RR /r̄/ pillar

Astonishingly rare, measured by the standard of other Hispano-Romance dialects, are the two suffixes -arru and -orru/-urru which constitute the series moored to RR. These elements seldom appear word-finally, performing their chief service as interfixes, as do invariably, we recall, -err-/-irr- (for a similar idiosyncrasy of -ardu and its vars. see Section 214.3 [d]):

(α) -arru: ñag-arr-u(du) 'excessively hard of pulp and green of color (of husk, skin, etc.), not fully ripened, insufficiently cooked' (speaking of fruits).

(β) -orru/-urru: es-bix-, espes-, espex-urr-iada '(milk) turning sour' (= es-birr-iada); es-ping-orr-et-iar 'to stain something with drops' (cf. ping-ar or -ay-ar 'to drip, droop,' pinga 'drop,' ping-ón 'drooping, shapeless' [of carelessly hung pieces of clothing], ping-an-eta 'pipe, spout,' ping-an-exu 'pipe draining a meager fountain, icicle').

[53]Observe that Western Asturian here shows, as one would expect, cobert-oira (Acevedo and Fernández), while Portuguese—apparently by way of a reverberation of the conflation of Lat. -ARIA and -ORIA on Castilian soil—offers cobert-eira.

(1) The SC /sk/ pillar

The dialect has a scant supply of semantically elusive formations in
-ascu, -escu, -iscu, -uescu (or their feminine counterparts),
attached to nominal stems. Some items function as diminutives, with the
customary referential bifurcation: 'small-sized' ~ 'young, of tender age';
occasionally one of these suffixes conveys a meteorological message
(weather conditions, etc.), as in Sp. nev-asca 'snowfall, blizzard,' Ptg. chuv-
(dial. chov-) isco 'drizzle.'

(α) b e r d - i - a s c a 'green twig,' f i y - a s c u 'stepson,' f o n t - a s c u,
- a s c a, even - a s q u - i n a 'small fountain,' p o l l - a s c u 'young rooster,'
'cub, whelp,' fig. 'boy trying to act like a grown-up'—a suffix performing
the same service, I agree with H. Lausberg, as does -ast(r)o elsewhere—in
rivalry, one is tempted to add, with -ato: Sp. poll-astro 'grown chicken,'
fig. 'sly fellow' vs. lebr-ato, -at-ón, -on-c-illo 'young hare, leveret.'

(β) c i - e s c u 'small particle of dust,' lit. 'of ashes.' A Western word
(*CINISCU) unaccountably gone astray in East-Central Asturias?[54] But cf.
Sp. cisco 'coal-dust, culm, slack,' fig. 'noisy wrangle, hubbub.'

(γ) f e c h - i s c u 'poor build or workmanship,' t o r b - i s c a beside
t o r b a 'slanting rain, accompanied by gales'; does e n - c e r r - i s c - á - s e
'to insist on sth., become obstinate' presuppose an adj. * c e r r - i s c u
paralleling Sp. cerr-il 'untamed, boorish, rough'? (I am reminded by D.
Catalán that Ast. cerrisco 'fiercely stubborn' ('terreno de difícil acceso,
persona que no admite razones en contra') and encerriscar 'to incite,
set on [dogs],' refl. 'to insist' are recorded by M. C. Díaz Castañón, El
bable del Cabo de Peñas [Oviedo, 1966]).

(δ) c i m - , c i n - u e s c a 'tight, plain knot' (cf. c i ñ - i r 'to gird').

(m) The SP pillar

This is a somewhat dubious pillar—conceivably at present an element "in
the making," as are in all likelihood the P-pillar and the F-pillar, with which
it shares the salient characteristic of labiality.[55] I see no excuse for ruling

---

[54] The loss of -n- here parallels the loss of -l- in m a z a - c u - a d a; see supra,
Section 211 (c) and n. 47.

[55] I must reserve the analysis of these nascent pillars for some future occasion on
account of several intrinsic complications. One infers a groping movement in the

it out, as long as neatly detachable -asp- and -ispa, attached to nouns and adjectives, lend themselves to minimal contrast:

(α) gay-asp-eru 'cheerful, in good mood' beside armar gay-ola 'to engage in merriment, in gaiety' (= Sp. armar juerga, jalea, holgorio).[56]

(β) fil-, fel-ispa 'fiber,' esp. that removed from beans in preparing meals; 'fibrous substance adhering to the hog's intestines' (= red-eña, adjoining the entruézanu).

---

direction of an F-pillar in examining gol-if-ar 'to scent, sniff' (which, genetically, is an amalgam of (a) gol-or 'stench'—cf. Sp. ol-or 'smell' and such related verb forms as coll. güele = huele 'it smells'—and (b) Sp. olfato '(sense of) smell'; or in dissecting Sp. piltra-ca, -fa 'skinny flesh, loot'; (pl.) 'scraps of food,' (Am.) 'rags, old clothes.' Again, even if one is forewarned by earlier exposure to medieval sources that farrapiu 'trace, remnant, residue' (orig. 'tatter, rag') echoes a compound (OSp. ferro-, farro-pea 'iron shackles attached to the feet [tearing the prisoners' clothes]') and that farrapiezu 'worn-out garment, rag' involves a widespread cross with pieza 'piece (of clothing),' cf. It. pezzo, there remains the eloquent fact of the diffusion of the p- forms to the historically unrelated family of FARĪNA 'flour' and FARRĀGŌ 'mixed fodder, mash,' witness farr-apes = far-iñes 'maize porridge' and the further and even more significant fact of the coexistence of gurria 'wrinkle' (= W.-Ast. engurria) and gurri-apu 'small, wrinkled apple,' 'puny person' (to say nothing of gurrión 'sparrow' = Sp. gorrión). Again, gorupa 'leather strap passing underneath a harnessed horse's tail' (i.e., one placed above the altafarra) may be an adaptation of Fr. croupe 'rump' (in the last analysis Frankish), but the anaptyxis and concurrent erratic voicing of /k-/ gives the word the appearance of an -upa derivative from a gor- kernel, and this -upa tends to enter into a secondary relationship with -ap(i)u and -apa (pl. -apes). I suspect that a nascent MP-pillar can also be isolated, since farr-amp-i-os 'flakes of snow' and the corresponding verb in -iar 'to snow' clearly call to mind the imagerial pattern of maize porridge (cf. Am. Engl. cornflakes). To the homorganic nasal before p one must assign some elaborative, emphatic, discriminatory, or sheer playful function; cf. the parallel expansion of -b- into -mb-: Sp. joroba beside gorr-, gurr-umba and Sp. jorob-ado 'hunchbacked' beside gurr-umb-u, -ín. This (still ill-defined) elaborative function of the epenthetic nasal must be rigorously distinguished from its anticipatory or echoing use determined by strictly phonic conditions.

[56] Certain side issues that happen to plague the language historian—association of Sp. gay-ola 'cage, jail, raised lookout in a vineyard,' from CAVEOLA, with the "adjusted" Provençalism or Catalanism gayo 'gay, bright, showy' (cf. Sp. gay-ar 'to trim with colored stripes')—ultimately either Frankish (Dauzat-Dubois-Mitterand) or Old High German (Gamillscheg)—can elicit only parenthetic mention in this context.

(n) The T̲ pillar

This pillar supports some of the most powerfully developed suffixes in Hispano-Romance, most of them with a diminutive slant and each boasting some additional overtone that sets it apart. One peculiarity of the arrangement is the lack of perfect symmetry in the masculine series, inasmuch as stressed a and i go with -u , while stressed e normally goes with -e : Hence -a t u and -i t u , but -e t e . However, a measure of leveling has apparently occurred, giving rise, at intervals, to -e t u .

(α) The core—i.e., the semantically closest-knit group of -a t u formations (with or without appeal to the -a r - interfix)—is provided by the young of animals and birds, exceptionally also by small and, by implication, young plants, e.g.: l l e b r - a t u 'young hare,' l l o b - a t u 'wolf cub,'[57] r o b l - a t u 'small oak,' p e g - a r - a t u 'young magpie,' beside self-explanatory l l e b r e , l l o b u , r o b l e , and p e g a (only the last-mentioned is listed and equated with Sp. urraca; fig. 'children's toy,' 'scarecrow'). The outer circle comprises miscellaneous derivatives from nouns, adjectives, and verbs, sometimes with interplay of -a̲r̲- or of the "parasitic" i̲ augment highly characteristic of Asturian; the meaning in this outer rim is derogatory rather than straight diminutive; e.g., c e g - a r - a t u 'shortsighted' beside, one gathers, c i e g u 'blind'; c u s p - i - a t u 'spit, expectoration' beside c u s p - i r 'to spew out'; f i s g - a t u and r e s g - a t u 'tear, rip,' perhaps also 'shred, tatter,' against the background of f i s g - a r and r e s g - a r , the latter inferrable from r e s g - ó n 'tear, tatter' (cf. Sp. rasg-a̲r̲); f l o r - i - a t u 'ordinary field flower'; ñ e s g - a t u 'scrap of cloth' (cf. ñ e s g - a r = Sp. nesg-a̲r̲ 'to gore, cut cloth on a bias'); m o ñ - a t u 'human excrement,' a word which comes closest to b o ñ - i c a 'bovine excrement,' cf. Sp. boñ̲-iga (also dial. moñ̲-iga) 'cow dung,' -igo 'pancake or patty (of cow dung).' Note that 'short-sighted' connotes a limited degree of blindness; that the nuance 'shred, tatter, scrap' also suggests 'smallness'

---

[57]Concerning l l o b - and its vars. l l a b - and l l e b - a t u 'clod or lump of earth not ploughed under' Krüger, in his review of Canellada (supra, n. 1 [p. 273]), offers noteworthy parallels, which encompass Murc. lob-ada 'ridge between furrows,' Cat. llob-ada 'spot in the field left untilled, pile of grass,' etc. and leave no doubt as to the agency of an animal metaphor. A faded metaphor, I incline to elaborate; how else can one justify the appearance of the l l a b - and l l e b - vars. (influenced by l l a b - i e g u 'plough,' l l e b - a n t - u 'elevation'?), which Krüger does not so much as attempt to explain? On the possibility of a differently slanted metaphoric use of l l o b u see my "Lexical Notes on the Western Leonese Dialect of Cabrera Alta," Language, XXX (1949), 437-446 (at 439), which form an adjunct to my review (ibid., 291-307) of M. C. Casado Lobato's Madrid dissertation.

as much as it evokes 'ruin, decay.'[58] Quite elusive is the function of - a t a
in f o g - a r - a t a beside f o g (u) - e r a 'bonfire,' alongside f u e u, h u e u
'fire'; one is vaguely reminded of Sp. llam-ar-ada 'flare-up, flush,' (fig.)
'outburst' beside llama 'flame' and is tempted to turn for parallels to those
words where the suffix suggests a 'split, cleavage, tear': f i s g - a t u, g a y -
a t u, r e s g - a t u; cf. f a r g - a t a 'breast,' 'décolleté.'

(β) - e t e, fem. - e t a: f o r q u - e t e, - e t a 'any forked stick,'
g u y - e t a 'shoelace with metal prongs' (beside f o r c a 'pitchfork,' g u y a
'needle'), m a c - e t e 'carpenter's wooden hammer' (cf. Sp. mazo 'hammer,'
presumably used in Cabranes as well); m o z q u - e t e, - e t a 'nick or dent
produced by a cut,' beside m u e s c a (with a "blind-alley reference" to
m u e z c a) 'dent in a cutting edge; piece of sth. that is being removed;
cavity left by the removal of that piece.' M u l - e t a 'stick or cane with a
curved handle' need not be native to Cabranes; cf. Sp. mul-eta 'crutch,' fig.
'prop, light lunch, etc.,' mul-et-illa 'pet phrase,' whose suffixal relationship to mul-o, -a 'mule' the geneticists find troublesome (cf. J. Corominas,
Dicc. crít. etim., III, 476a). On d e f o l g u - e t a see under (h), supra.
Masc. - e t u, no doubt analogical (extracted on the model of - i t u / - i t a,
etc.; also represented in Asturian toponymy), presides over the rise of
f o c - e t u beside - e t e 'small sickle' (= s e g - a ñ u; cf. Sp. hoz, Ptg.
fouce). Note also g o b - e t u 'bent, curved' (adj.) alongside - e t a 'curved
pruning knife,' cf. Sp. agob-i-ar 'to bow, weigh down, overburden,' lit. 'to
curve' (R. J. Cuervo).

(γ) - i t u, - i t a: (mi)g - a r - i t u 'piece of bread or cake' (pp. 234,
267). The comparative rarity here of this diminutive suffix, so overwhelm-
ingly strong in other varieties of Hispano-Romance—though little used in
Castilian before the seventeenth century—may be one reason for the optional
apheresis of the opening syllable. The change of gender, the insertion of
- a r - (whose initial function may have been to produce a suitable wedge
between the i's in two successive syllables), plus the tendential apheresis
make g a r i t u a truly unrecognizable derivative of m i g a 'bit, crumb,
soft part of bread.' Supporting examples: f l o r - i t u 'ordinary flower,'
f o r g u - i t a 'wood-shaving' (contrastable with f o r g - a x a, - (u) i x a
'id.'), g o r g - o l - i t u 'trill' (= Sp. gorg-ol-ito) beside g o r g -, g u r g -
u t - a r 'to utter, mutter, mumble' (Rato: -ut-ir).

---

[58]Some special cases must be set aside. Thus, g o l - i - a t u 'unspecifiable smell'
is patently a blend of g o l - o r 'smell' and learned Sp. olfato '(sense of) smell,' based
on OLFACTUM 'scenting-out, detection'; f i l i - a t u 'inspector's office' may be a distortion of (semilearned) Sp. fiel-ato.

(o) The X /š/ pillar

The few nominal formations in -a x u / -a x a, -e x u, -i x a, and
-o x u / -o x a, derived from nouns and adjectives, may relate to a substance,
a growth, a spot. This semantic haziness is a distinctive feature of these
suffixes, borrowed as fixed parts of lexical units from such dialects as have
a /š/ solidly built into their sound system. As if to complicate matters,
-a x u has established a side-connection with -a x e, the counterpart of
Sp. -aje, as in f e r r a - x e 'set of six nails driven into each of the three
"feet" of a wooden shoe'; cf. f a r d - a x u 'drubbing, thrashing' (lit. 'bag-
ful'?—note the link to f a r d - e l a 'knapsack, haversack' and to Sp. fardo
'bundle') as against Rato's -axe, echoing medieval usage).

(α) f o r g - a x a 'wood-shaving,' alternating with -(u)i x a, -(u)i t a.

(β) p i n g - a n - e x u 'pipe draining a meager fountain, icicle'; cf.
f o r c - e x - u d u 'husky,' a transparent adaptation of Sp. forc-ej-udo (familiar
from Sayagués).

(γ) c l a r - i x a 'patch of slightly misty brightness,' cf. f o l - i x a 'obstrep-
erous gaiety, noisy merriment'—probably Sp. fol-ía 'light, popular music' in
disguise (cf. E. fool-ery), and s a n - i x - u e l a 'leech,' in fairly close approximation to Sp. sangu-ij-uela.

(δ) m a t - o x u 'small thicket' (cf. Sp. mat-orr-al for the meaning and the
phytonym mat-ojo 'glasswort,' also 'bush,' in general, for the form);
m i e l - o x a 'something as sweet as honey' (but Sp. milhojas 'puff-pastry'
seems to involve mil 'thousand' rather than miel 'honey'; note the semantic
contrast to the French phytonym mille-feuille 'milfoil, yarrow').

(p) The Y /j/ pillar

The native derivatives in -a y u, -e y u, -i y u, and -o y u / -u y u
form a network comparable and cognate to Sp. -ajo, -ejo, -ijo, -ojo/-ujo
and to Ptg. -alho, etc.; the real complication of this wing of the suffixal
structure of the Cabraniego dialect is rooted in the coexistence of native
-a y u and borrowed -a x u, etc. Semantically, the /j/ suffixes are somewhat more sharply contoured than are their borrowed counterparts.

(α) -a y u is distinctly commiserative or pejorative: c i n t - a y a 'bad,
useless ribbon or band' (doubtless beside c i n t a); c o c - i - a y u 'mixed
vegetables and offals cooked for the hogs' (related to c o c - e r 'to cook,
leave chestnut wood floating in the river' [i.e., prepare it, etc.); f o n d - i g -
a y u (or -a y - a d a) 'lowland, bottom land' (cf. Sp. hond-on-ada), (topon.)

font-ayu 'thin, feeble stream of water,' beside huente and no doubt
fuente (see Canellada, pp. 15f.); mig-aya 'crumb, bit' (beside miga
'soft part of bread,' not expressly recorded; cf. Sp. miga-ja); trip-ayu
'worthless gut'—probably of no use in preparing sausages and blood pudding
—from tripu, the counterpart of Sp. tripa.

(β) -eyu is diminutive-derogatory: felp-eyu 'loosely hanging tatter'
and felp-ey-ón 'ragged, shabby, carelessly dressed,' cf. Sp. felpa 'plush.'

(γ) -iyu: bot-iya 'black-clayed, two-handled pot with a hole, used
in churning butter' (cf. Sp. bot-ija 'earthen jug'), related to the bot- stem
('container') echoed by bot-iellu 'stomach, esp. an animal's' (llená-l
bot-iellu 'to stuff oneself').

(δ) -oyu —typically a suffixoid: fen-, cen-oyu 'fern' (= Sp. hin-ojo),
god-oyu 'bundle of clothes' (= god-ob-iellu), gorg-uy-os 'pimples'
(cf. Ptg. borb-ulh-as; an "expressive" word).

(q) The Z /θ/ pillar

This pillar, strongly entrenched in the dialect, is represented by two
flourishing suffixes, -azu and -izu, as well as by their feminine
counterparts.

(α) -azu, -aza form nouns whose meaning to this day may disclose
an intermediate adjectival stage; thus, per-aza, lit. 'pearlike, pear-
shaped,' applying as it does to a locally favored species of apple, has preserved something of the original sequence mazana per-aza. Completely independent of the main uses of -azu, -aza —in terms of their
separate origins as well as in the context of their present-day mutual
relationships—is the invariably masc. -azu used as a fanciful designation
of blows and other sudden and sometimes noisy movements—in keen rivalry
with -ón, -atu, and -ada;[59] the primitive is either the instrument
wielded (αα) or the part of the body aimed at (ββ), while in a residue of cases
the radical's original contour has been badly distorted (γγ)—quite apart from
a small stock of figurative uses (δδ):

(αα) berd-i-ag-azu 'blow with a stick' (berd-i-agu); berd-
i-asc-azu 'blow with a green twig' (berd-i-asca = Sp. verd-asca);
calc-añ-ar-azu 'kick with the heel' (calc-añ-ar, as in Spanish?),

---

[59] For details see my article "The Two Sources of the Hispanic Suffix -azo, -aço,"
Language, XXXV (1959), 193-258, esp. 194-206.

as against c a l c - a ñ - a z u 'hole in the ground made by the third "foot" of one's wooden shoe' and c a l c - a ñ - ó n 'sprain of one's foot'; g a t - u ñ - a z u 'scratch' (cf. g a t - , g a r d - u ñ a 'sharp-toothed animal trap'; note Sp. gard-uña 'stone marten').

(ββ) c a l a m u r n - i - a z u 'hard blow on one's head' (to ascertain the primitive, akin to coll. Sp. calamorra 'head,' observe synonymous c a l a - m u r n - i - ó n); g o c h - a z u 'fall, tumble (on one's tummy)' beside g o c h u 'hog, navel.' In m a n - c o r n - i - a z u beside m a n - c u r n - i u 'any blow; whack, damage' the hand may, by way of exception, represent both the weapon and the part of the anatomy afflicted.

(γγ) s o f r o n - a z u 'rude repartee, public display of contempt' is unanalyzable except for those trained historically or familiar with Sp. so-fren-ada 'sudden checking of a horse' (based on freno 'bridle') > 'severe reprimand.'

(δδ) r a m - a l - a z u 'spell of madness,' incomprehensible as to struc- ture without reference to the more technical meaning: 'sudden emergence of a branchlike venature ("ramo de sangre") in the eye'; s o r b - i - a t - a z u 'loud noise made in sipping' beside s o r b - i - a t u 'small sip,' pre- sumably based on the local representative of Sp. sorbo 'sip, gulp, swallow' rather than on the underlying verb.

By way of exception - a z u seems to match Sp. -azgo, as in m a y o r - a z u = mayor-azgo '(right of, entailed estate descending by) primo- geniture.'

(β) - i z u performs two rather neatly distinguishable services:

(αα) It is attached to past participles—in competition with - i e g u (see G-pillar, under [d] supra)—to produce a strictly adjectival series of formations. The verbal adjectives at issue ordinarily denote lasting qualities flowing from an action, thus: a - f a y - a - í z u 'bobbing up all the time, apt to be met (seemingly) by chance'—reminiscent of Sp. en- contr-ad-izo—beside a f a y - á - s e 'to find oneself well off or comfortably installed' (cf. Sp. hall-ar); a - f o g - a - í z u (= - a d - i e g u) 'easily drowned or stifled; sinkable, non-floating,' presumably beside a - f o g - a r (cf. Sp. a-hog-ar 'to drown, smother'); a - t o p - a - í z u 'snug, comfortable' beside a - t o p - á - s e , a synonym of a - f a y - á - s e (cf. Sp. top-ar 'to butt, bump, run into, encounter by chance').

(ββ) It joins nominal stems and an occasional primary adjective to pro- duce secondary adjectives which, in turn, easily lend themselves to nomi- nalization: e m b e r n - i z u 'hibernal,' specifically e m - b e r n - i c e s 'potatoes harvested in winter'—best analyzed as an imported Castilianism (cf. Sp. invern-izo) in view of the imperfect match with the local word for 'winter' (i b i e r n u); g a s t - i z u 'spendthrift' (surely supported by g a s t - a r 'to waste'); m e d - , m e l - , and m e m - e r - i z u 'sparrow-like bird, with greenish feathers, known for laying seven eggs,' from a primitive that remains to be ascertained (any connection with m i e l r u = Sp. mirlo 'blackbird'?); p o d r - i z u 'smell of sth. rotten,' beside a cluster of readily decomposable formations in - é n, - i g - a ñ u, and - i g - a ñ - a r involving p o d r - e 'putrid.'[60]

212. Verbal suffixes entering into vocalic gamuts.

These clusters, relatively few, are organized exactly like their nominal counterparts, each characterized by a mono- or a bi-phonemic consonant pillar and by a vocalic gamut comprising a minimum of two contrastable vowels. The stems involved in these interplays are, typically, verbal; in some instances, there arises the possibility of a secondary association of the derivative with a noun as well; through further development of this marginal possibility, the exceptional extraction of a verb marked by one of these suffixes from a strictly nominal stem has also been observed. (One must, from the start, exclude those cases where the suffix formed part and parcel of the noun on which the verb hierarchically depends; thus, e s - c a r a b - i c - a r 'to poke, clean a cavity' involves a standard derivative in - a r from e s - c a r a b - i c u 'little poking-stick,' fig. 'restless, meddlesome person.')

(a) The C /k/ pillar

One can set off very sharply the two series of - i c a r and - u c a r verbs, which match quite closely the respective groups of nouns in - i c u / - i c a and - u c u / - u c a.

(α) Verbs in - i c - a r, which may be extracted from verbal or, more sparingly, from nominal stems, indicate processes or activities judged with amusement or mild irony. (It will be remembered that in the nominal domain the segment - i c - suggests smallness blended with daintiness and exquisiteness. Thus, c a x - i n a refers to any 'small box,' c a x - i q u - i n a to a 'pretty

---

[60]Not to be confused with - i z a is - i s a, as in p o b i s a 'minute particles of dust (produced by seeds or birds), fine ashes floating around a flame'—beside p o l b o r - e u 'dust cloud,' the counterpart of Sp. polv-ar-eda. P o b - i s a reminds one of OSp. cen-isas 'ashes,' mod. -izas (Canellada omits its dialectal equivalent).

little box'; c e r - i c a or - i q u - i n a designates the smallest locally known
bird, which it is sinful to kill, etc.) The semantic ingredient of 'smallness'
resolves itself, when transferred to the realm of verbs, into 'slowness,'
'gentleness, delicacy,' 'hesitation, lack of zest,' 'spacing-out along the axis
of time,' 'breaking-down a continuum into isolable vibrations,' and the like,
unless of course the smallness attaches to the quantifiable amounts of work
performed. Thus, to start with verbal stems, c o c - i c - a r is 'to cook slowly
and cautiously' (as against c o c - e r); c o m - i c - a r is 'to eat little, as
when one is not hungry' (as against c o m - e r); c o s - i c - a r is 'to sew
listlessly or with interruptions' (as against c o s - e r); l l o b - i c - a r is
'to drizzle' (as against, presumably, l l o b - e r 'to rain'). The last item is
likewise associable with l l o b - i u 'rain'; ñ e b - i c - a r , which suggests a
slow falling of snowflakes, has a divided loyalty to ñ e b - a r 'to snow' (un-
listed, but readily conjecturable) and ñ (i) e b e 'snow.' Strictly nominal in
its roots is c a ñ - i c - a r , refl. 'to grasp a tree branch and swing or let
oneself fall,' tr. 'to rock' (a cradle), 'make something reel, totter, vibrate,'
clearly related to c a ñ a 'branch,' with a vaguely identified masculine counterpart in - u . The author records no comparable derivative from c a - e r 'to
fall,' but one gathers from c a - i c - ó n 'one who treads unsteadily' (Rato y
Hevia: 'coward') that there must also exist, or until recently have existed,
the matching verb c a - i c - a r , since - i c - is unlikely to function merely
as an antihiatic interfix, as does - i r - (probably a by-form of - e r -) in
c a - i r - ó n 'abyss, ravine, slope.'

(β) Verbs in - u c - a r are likewise characterized by their suggestion of
'lack of intensity,' but there is often a perceptible emphasis on 'futility, frus-
tration, scattering of effort, frittering-away of time, dearth of accomplish-
ment, meagerness of reward,' cf. c e n - u c - a r , not only 'to have a light
supper, a supper snack,' but also 'to consume food that is barely nourishing';
similarly m e r e n d - u c - a r 'to have an extra-light lunch,' p a ñ - u c - a r
'to grasp sth. many times and with scant results, or to grasp few things, or
to grasp with little eagerness'; t r a b a y - u c - a r 'to work little, or to
squander one's energy on trivial things demanding no effort.' One is tempted
to relate e s - c a n - u c - a r 'to chew off the meat attached to the bones'
either to c a n - i l 'canine tooth' or, even better (this is D. Catalán's choice),
to Ast. cañá = cañada 'marrow' (cf. Sp. caña, canilla 'long bone'). The choice
of - i c a r vs. - u c a r may not be entirely controlled by semantic content.
In e n - f r i - u c - a r 'to turn a bit chilly' (speaking of the weather) the selec-
tion of - i c - would have been phonotactically hazardous.

(b) The SC /sk/ pillar

(α) The -i s c - variant is observable in e n - c e r r - i s c - á - s e 'to engage or persist in, to insist on,' with an overtone of 'stubbornness' (cf. Sp. cerr-il 'rough, untamed, boorish').

(β) A perfect illustration of -u s c - is r i ñ - u s c - a r 'to demur, quarrel mildly' beside r i ñ - i r 'to fight, fall out, quarrel.' The same element is a mere suffixoid in c h a m b - u s c - a r 'to singe, scorch' on account of the severe isolation of the stem. Sp. cham-usc-ar, on the other hand, is contrastable with cham-ar-(asc)a 'brush fire'; cham-izo 'half-burned tree' and -iza 'brush used as firewood,' -ic-era 'strip of burned woodland'; also, it boasts offshoots, such as cham-usc-o 'singeing,' -usqu-ina 'id.,' (coll.) 'row, quarrel.'

(c) The X /š/ pillar

The aggregate of the verbs at issue constitutes a borderline case, because the contrast between - e x - a r and - o x - a r / - u x - a r is anything but neat on the semantic side—doubtless a consequence of their thoroughly disparate backgrounds.[61] It is conceivable, however, that through gradual convergence the distance is being shortened and will eventually be bridged:

(α) The - e x - component of - e x - a r is endowed with no clear meaning of its own except the suggestion of 'rhythmically spaced repetition.' This iterative overtone is perceptible in onomatopoeic c a c a r - e x - a r 'to cackle' (Sp. cacar-e-ar) and in d e b a n - e x - a r 'to move around a lot; to hustle, bustle, go back and forth' (cf. Sp. devan-ar 'to wind, spool, roll').

(β) The - o x - / - u x - component of e s - b a t - o x - a r , - u x - a r 'to splash water and mud, moving through puddles' (Acevedo and Fernández: 'to stir or shake water in a container') has the overtone of 'coarseness' peculiar to numerous Romance o- suffixes.

(d) The Y /j/ pillar

(α) In most instances - a y - a r cannot be sharply individuated as a verbal suffix. Thus, (d) e s - m i g - a y - a r 'to break into crumbs' lends itself to association with both m i g a and m i g - a y a ; e s - b a b - a y - á - s e (already

[61]Genetically, - e x a r belongs with Gal. -exar, Ptg. -ejar < Gr.-Lat. -IDIĀRE, which has also left a few deposits in Spanish (cf. forc-ej-ar, -ear 'to struggle, contend'). Conversely, - o x - a r marks borrowings from central dialects or from standard speech, where -oj- reflects -UCULU. The native Spanish product of -IDIĀRE is -ear (= Ast. -iar); the native Asturian outgrowth of -UCULU is - o y u or - u y u.

known from Rato y Hevia and from Acevedo and Fernández) is not only a
synonym of babá-se 'to drip' (slaver, speaking of infants; liquids, speaking of containers; melted wax, speaking of candles), but also a member of
the subfamily of bab-aya 'drivel,' -ay-ar 'to engage in silly talk,'
-ayu 'foolish,' -ay-ada 'stupidity,' -ay-osu 'slobbery'; es-carab-
ay-ar 'to scrawl, botch a drawing' flanks es-carab-ayu 'botched
drawing, crude picture, line carelessly drawn'; es-colg-ay-ar 'to hang
down in tatters,' p. ptc. -ay-au 'walking around, feeble and depressed,'
beside colg-ayu 'rag, tatter' suggested by its congener Sp. colg-ajo (cf.
colg-ar 'to hang') if not expressly recorded. A neat example, however, is
provided by es-coc-i-ay-ar 'to boil or cook [too] slowly; to spoil or
ruin a dinner' (alongside coc-er), with a sharply derogatory overtone.

(β) Of -oy-ar, var. -uy-ar at least one clear-cut example can be
cited: es-bat-oy-ar (or -uy-ar, with no semantic differentiation)
'to whip or churn a liquid, esp. cream, to produce butter' beside bat-ir 'to
beat,' whose existence and semantic specialization one infers from Spanish.
Note the narrow gap separating this (native) verb from its (imported) doublet
in -ox-ar, -ux-ar (supra, under [c]).

(e) The Z /θ/ pillar

The analysis of this case is beset with particular difficulties, in part on
account of the opaqueness of some apparently relevant formations, in part
because the descriptivist must beware of any historical prejudice.[62]

(α) Ast. -izar is, at first glance, so closely reminiscent of semilearned
Sp. -izar (baut-izar 'to baptize,' amen-izar 'to make pleasant, add charm to,'
suav-izar 'to ease, soften, sweeten, tone down')—which distinctly enters into
no vocalic gamut—that one begins to suspect its separate roots and function
only by dint of observation. As an altogether vernacular suffix it flourishes
in such Cabraniego verbs as camp-iz-á-se 'to become covered with
grass' (beside campu 'field'), em-pap-iz-ar (or -iell-ar) 'to
choke on' (cf. pap-au 'gulp, swallow,' pap-ar-au 'mouthful'), en-cerr-
iz-ar 'to sick, stir up, egg on' (cf. en-cerr-isc-ar, supra, under [b]).

(β) A possible example of -uz-ar can be deduced from en-gorg-uz-
au 'bent over, crouching, cowering (with the body leaning forward).'

[62]Learned -izar in Spanish is the counterpart of vernacular -ear (see n. 61, supra)
and matches Fr. -iser, Engl. -ize or -ise, etc. The varieties of -iz-ar, and -uz-
ar that tend to yield gamuts match nominal formations in -izu (-iciu) and -uzu
(-uciu) and are ultimately traceable to -ÍCEU and -ŪCEU.

(f) Dubious pillars

Perhaps the most arresting feature of the Cabraniego material here on display is the fact that several pillars seem to be crystallizing before our eyes. Is it advisable to posit the separate existence of a T̲-pillar? Perhaps so; consider the widespread presence of verbs in - o t - i - a r (= Sp. -ot-ear), ordinarily in conjunction with some appropriate prefix, such as (e s) - l l a b - o t - i - a r 'to wash repeatedly or lightly' (beside self-explanatory l l a b - a r , surrounded by a phalanx of derivatives); or e s - f r e g - o t - i - a r 'to (sc)rub, scour repeatedly, or with a light touch' (beside e s - f r e g - a r 'to rub hard, esp. the maize cob, so as to remove the grains from it' and e s - f r e g - u y - a r 'to crumb, crumble'), also e s - p i c - o t - i - a r   (a) 'to pick at a fruit' (speaking of a bird, beside p i c u 'beak, bill'), (b) 'to cut off the corners of a handkerchief' (alongside p i c u 'tip, sharp point'): - o t - i - a r unmis-takably resolves a durative action into a staccato-like succession of short movements, or shears that action of any strength and intensity. If we place alongside that bundle of pointillistic verbs an item like e s - g a r - i t - a r 'to break into small pieces,' which owes its allegiance to apheresized (m i) g - a r - i t u (and which maintains cross-connections to its congeners and syno-nyms e s - m i g - a y - a r , - u y - a r), then we recognize, against a back-ground of striking semantic affinity, an incipient - i t - a r suffixoid. Jointly, - o t - i - a r and - i t - a r meet all the requirements for eventual coalescence into a vocalic gamut, with marked potentialities of further expansion.

Again, - o p - i - a r occurs just too frequently not to arouse one's suspi-cion; typically, it prevails (not unlike - o t - i - a r) in parasynthetic verbs ushered in by e s - ; cf. e s - c a l d - o p - i - a r 'to pour too much sauce or gravy on a dish, spoiling it in the process' beside e s - c a l d - a r 'to warm up, feed the poultry a kind of warm porridge' (refl. 'to get excited, go crazy, etc.'); e s - c a z - o p - i - a r 'to mess up, disturb, turn upside down, meddle inopportunely,' in the close vicinity of e s - c a z - o p - (i) e l l - a r 'to overdo the stirring of food' (related to e s - c a z - a r 'to remove the hard crust from hoofs of slaughtered animals by exposing it to fire'?); e s - g u i l - o p - i - a r 'to climb nimbly up a tree' flanking e s - g u i l - a r 'to climb,' - ó n 'tree-climbing bird, the size of a sparrow.' Encouraged by this rich haul, one is inclined to postulate an autonomous verbal P̲-pillar at the first sight of, say, suffixal - a p - ; little surprise is caused by the discovery of e s - g a r r - a p - e t - a u 'wearing a torn outfit,' a word in which one finds enmeshed stray ele-ments of f a r r - a p - i - u 'rest, remnant' (cf. Sp. har-apo 'tatter') and - a p - i e z - u 'old rag or garment,' on the one hand, and of g a r r - a r 'to seize, grasp' (cf. Sp. a-garr-ar matching garra 'claw'), on the other.

From here, the path leads to the even more controversial F-pillar, as in
es-garr-af-ar 'to wear a torn suit' and es-garr-af-á-se, a synonym of es-farr-ap-á-se 'to lose shape, grow weak, disappear from
excess of softness.'

To strike out in another direction: Straddling the nascent P- and T-pillars
alike are the twin formations es-ñal-op-i-ar and es-ñal-ot-ar 'to
flutter, flap the wings'[63] (cf. Sp. al-et-ar, re-vol-ot-e-ar, similarly architectured), related to Sp. nid-al, dial. ni-al, ñal 'nest (egg),' cf. ni-ego 'nest-
ling.'

Finally, the coexistence of (a) -añ-ar, as in (es)-mord-ig-añ-ar
'to nibble, gnaw at' (vs. es-morg-añ-ar 'to open one's mouth wide, split
one's sides with laughter'); (b) -iñ-ar, as in es-tof-iñ-ar 'to beat,
slap, tarnish, discredit' (cf. tof-iñu 'piqued, irritated person,' en-tof-
iñ-á-se 'to get angry'); and (c) -uñ-ar, as in mas-uñ-ar 'to finger,'
etc. makes the existence of an Ñ-pillar not implausible.

One can easily be seduced into going too far along this path. It is, at first
glance, tempting to posit an NT-pillar on the strength of a handful of -ant-
ar and -ent-ar verbs, but the counsel of wisdom is to refrain from doing
so. There do exist in Cabraniego some verbs structured like en-gaf-ent-
ar 'to make sore, poison'—which, judging from western parallels, need not
presuppose any such immediate antecedent as *gaf-ientu, but may be
directly linked to gafu 'leprous, claw-handed.'[64] But if -ent-ar is productive, -ant-ar has become a petrifact in Hispano-Romance (cf. Sp.
a-mam-ant-ar 'to suckle, nurse,' lev-ant-ar 'to lift'), a circumstance inimi-
cal to the crystallization of a vocalic gamut. Other arguments against the
supposition of an NT-pillar are the lack of any semantic contrast between
-ant-ar and -ent-ar and the phonetic meagerness of the contrast $/a/$:
$/e/$, as against, say, $/i/$: $/u/$, or $/a/$: $/i/$, or $/a/$: $/u/$, or $/a/$: $/i/$: $/u/$.[65]

---

[63]The growing near-synonymy of -ot-iar and -op-iar raises the question
whether their eventual distribution may not hinge on a kind of preventive consonant
dissimilation of the same type as Sp. -al : -ar, Fr. -eul : -euil, etc.; see K. Togeby's
perceptive comments in his paper, "Qu'est-ce que la dissimilation?," Romance
Philology, XVII (1963-64), 642-667, esp. 649, and in a very recent book review: Acta
Linguistica Hafniensia, XI (1968), 227f.

[64]On the family of Sp. gafo see the concluding pages of my article "La familia
léxica lazerar, laz(d)rar, lazeria; estudios de paleontología lingüística," Nueva Revista de Filología Hispánica, VI (1952), 209-276; on the verbal suffix -ent-ar and its
relation to -(i)ento see the remarks in Studies in Philology, XXXVIII (1941), 453, and
in Language, XVIII (1942), 58f.

[65]The discrepant degrees of vitality of -ant-ar and -ent-ar in Hispano-Romance
are due to a simple case of asymmetry: -ant-ar depended for nourishment on -ant

213. A new classification of Romance derivational suffixes?

It is a commonplace of Romance linguistics—chiefly in its diachronic dimension, yet to some extent also in the synchronic projection of facts— that all derivational suffixes fall into two major groups: those still productive and those fossilized, even if clearly recognizable by untutored speakers. (Scholars have learned to make allowances for two additional categories marginally represented: semi-extinct suffixes, apt to be revived occasionally in pretentious discourse—cf. Engl. -dom and -hood—and mere relics, identifiable solely through historico-comparative analysis, while representing "deadwood" to the layman.) This traditional division has its measure of justification for certain types of analysis and its validity need not here be challenged. Significantly, there have at all times existed rival classifications (e.g., those using as prime dividers such dichotomies as vernacular vs. learned, or nominal vs. verbal), and the main purpose of this exploratory paper has been, of all goals, to draw attention to the advantage of letting another, long neglected, division for once occupy the center of the stage.

In far more dramatic fashion than does the highly conventionalized literary language, an unshackled dialect like Cabraniego attunes our ear to the basic difference between such suffixes as are structurally isolated (e.g., adj. -osu, nom. -mientu, verb. -ec-er) and others that fall, or are on their way to falling, into vocalic gamuts. Since this kind of patterning is a living force, there is a constant latent challenge for speakers to fill "empty pigeonholes" in the shorter gamuts, to press into service suitable new pillars (cf. P, F, etc.), and to nuance the semantic load of each unit, until the characteristic message conveyed by the consonant and the playful, emotional overtone suggested by the vowel can be exhibited to best advantage. Hence the extraordinary dosage of originality and vitality that can be detected in these morphemes and in the words into which they enter. This constant ebullience of the material, fluidity of usage, and ceaseless creativity of the speakers toying with new ideas has a sparkle about it which must be identified as a very different quality from the mere productivity of unaligned, isolated suffixes. The resemblance of this state of affairs to the imaginative distinction drawn by Prague-style phonologists between "integrated phonemes" and "unintegrated phonemes" is obvious and need not be labored.

Because our dialect's derivational morphemes unintegrated into gamuts show such a narrow edge of originality, they lend themselves to fairly cursory inventorying.

---

alone, -ent-ar absorbed strength from both participial -(i)ente and purely adjectival -(i)ento, cf. Lat. -(UL)ENTUS. The latter prospered in the Western section of the Peninsula, while the fortune of the present participles declined everywhere.

214. Unintegrated derivational suffixes.

These suffixes, which are here examined rather summarily—for the sake of completeness and also for the contrast they afford to those entering into gamuts—pose a major classificatory problem. Should they be inventoried in random fashion (say, in alphabetic order)? Can one, alternatively, set up certain formal norms for the grouping of the miscellaneous items (e.g., the total of phonemes involved, or the number of consonants, or certain distinctive features of sound)? Is it advisable to array them on the basis of meaning or function?

Granted the deemphasis here deliberately placed on this residual slice of the material, it seems permissible to advocate a compromise solution. We shall use as major classifier functional (grammatical) considerations, setting off formations (a) predominantly adjectival and (b) substantival (i.e., both adjectival and nominal) from those (c) strictly nominal, and all three categories from those (d) verbal and (e) adverbial. Of these smaller groupings only (c) easily lends itself to further subdivision, on a mixed functional-semantic basis (adjectival and verbal abstracts, etc.). Each smallest unit thus analytically arrived at will be organized in alphabetic, i.e., conventional, sequence.

214.1. Purely (or preeminently) adjectival suffixes.

The adjectival suffixes -ientu, -iondu, and -osu deserve mention.

(a) Characteristically (though far from exclusively) western is -ientu (by-form -entu after palatal consonants, esp. after /ɲ/): fam-ientu 'hungry' (= es-fam-i-au; Rato y Hevia, Acevedo and Fernández favor fam-i-ón, the latter also record -ento); fariñ-entu 'floury, mealy' (beside -osu and -ón, the last-mentioned displaying secondary meanings as well: 'porridge-fancier,' 'too soft for work or for endurance of pain'); ferr-uñ-entu (= furr-uñ-osu, with labialization of the first vowel) 'rusty'; maf-ientu 'moldy, musty' (alongside maf-ecer 'to turn moldy'; the primitive mafa is credited with the meaning 'sticky substance adhering to unwashed containers, to undrained pools, and to teeth left uncleaned'); maur-ientu, allegedly a synonym of the last-mentioned adjective, lit. 'overripe' (cf. Sp. maduro). The same sound sequence functions as a mere suffixoid in engr-, ingr-ientu 'reddened' (by exposure to fire, after a coughing spell, etc.).

(b) Rare (in terms of lexical frequency and of incidence alike) and semantically narrow is -iondu, referring to flavors and smells: berr-iondu 'tasting like a germinated seed or fruit' (Sp. verr-iondo 'rutting, in heat;

withered' is etymologically more transparent), cf. Section 111, supra; f e d -
i o n d u (adj.) 'malodorous'; (noun) 'name of white-blossomed plant exuding
a stench,' beside f e d - e r 'to stink,' - o r 'stench.'

(c) Very common and, due to its wide range, referentially neutral is
- o s u : f o n g - o s u (= - ó n) 'spongy, fluffy' (speaking of excessively soft
ground or obese persons), beside f o n g u 'mushroom' conjecturable from
Sp. hongo; f o r o ñ - o s u (= a - f o r o ñ - a u) 'mothy, worm-eaten, under-
mined' (the -rr- in Rato y Hevia's counterpart forroñ-oso betrays inter-
ference of the local word for 'rust'), cf. f o r - o ñ u , - u ñ u 'dust made by
wood borer'; f u r r - u ñ - o s u 'rusty' beside - u ñ u 'rust'; (e n -) g u e d e y -
o s u 'equipped with (e n) g u e d e y o s , i.e., 'sth. fit for hooking up, catching
on, tangling up, confusing, dallying with' (cf. Sp. guedeja 'long hair'); l l a m -
a r g - o s u (= - i z u) 'swamplike' beside l l a m - a r g - a , - a l 'ground
turned into a puddle' (cf. Sp. lama 'mud, slime, ooze').

As one gathers from our parenthetic comments, these unintegrated suffixes
are chiefly pitted in competition with integrated a — a u , e s — a u , and
- ó n .

214.2. Suffixes straddling the form-classes of adjectives and nouns.

The two most prominent among such suffixes so far omitted are - e r u
and - a d o r / - i d o r , along with the former's feminine counterpart:

(a) - e r u has produced a handful of purely relational adjectives that may
qualify an inanimate noun, e.g., l l i b i - e r u 'light and loose' (speaking of
soil), comparable to Sp. livi-ano, It. leggi-adro, etc.; but ordinarily it de-
scribes an animal or a human, singling out his particular skill or leaning
(hankering, concern): c a c - e r u 'given to hunting, prowling, pursuing'
(beside, one is certain, c a z a 'hunt, chase'); c a c i p (l) - e r u 'plotting,
intriguing, setting snares,' beside (e s -) c a c i p (l) - a r 'to gossip, entrap';
m a n t e g (u) - e r a '(cow) producing a lot of buttermilk' (= W.-Ast. manteigu-
eira), in the retinue of m a n t - e g a 'butter' (cf. m a n t e g - ó n 'softish,
spineless').

One can best do justice to the thick bundle of nominal functions of
- e r u by considering separately the masculine and the feminine varieties.
The former prevails (a) in designations of agents (i.e., manufacturers or
collectors as well as sellers of certain objects or products), e.g., a b l a n -
e r u 'seller of hazelnuts' (beside a b l a - n a), g o x - e r u 'manufacturer
of hampers made of unpolished rods' (beside g o x a), 'manufacturer of
wicker baskets' (beside g o x u), m a d r - e ñ - e r u 'manufacturer or seller
of wooden shoes' (alongside m a d r - e ñ a); and (b) in names of tools (broadly
interpreted), e.g., g u y - e r u 'needle cushion' (cf. g u y a 'needle,' the cog-

nate of Sp. aguja) and m a z o r g u - e r u 'instrument for filling a m a z o r g a (= Sp. mazorca), i.e., a reel or bobbin in a sewing machine.'

The feminine variety also refers to all sorts of tools and containers, e.g., c o l l - e r a 'wooden shackle used to attach a cow to its manger' beside c u e l l u 'neck' (note the phrase t e n e r   e n   c u e l l a 'to hold a baby in one's arms'), g u e d e y - e r a 'device for keeping sth. entrapped, fastened, hooked' (beside aforecited g u e d e y - u), m a s - e i r a 'kneading trough, box used in the apple press' (cf. m a s a 'dough,' omitted on account of its obviousness), t o r t - e r a 'small iron shovel used in baking a cake' (either t o r t a, taken for granted by the author, or, if a smaller cake is involved, t o r t u).

But the feminine boasts many more uses. It may refer to a season, or to seasonal weather (cf. Sp. tempor-ada): e m - b e r n - e r a, a less than smooth fit for i b i e r n u 'winter'; or it characterizes the word as a phytonym: e d r - e r a 'ivy' (cf. Sp. hiedra), 'ivy-like parasite attacking the maize plant'; or it is attached to an adjective to designate an infirmity or a physical defect: b (i) e y - e r a 'old age' (beside b i e y u 'old'), cf. Sp. sord-era 'deafness,' It. vecchi-aia 'old age.'

Semantically, the suffix - d o r parallels - e r u by producing agentives from verbal rather than from nominal stems. Structurally, however, it pertains to the exiguous group of derivational morphemes ushered in not by a stressed vowel, but by a consonant, much as are - d á and - m i e n t u (see Section 210). In the case of - d o r this consonant is linked to the stem by means of an unstressed vowel (a or i) whose choice is controlled solely by the conjugation class of the given verb and which, as a result, carries no message of its own. Unstressed vowels reduced to this subordinate function fall into no truly meaningful gamut, in terms of either the volume of information conveyed or of the degree of creativity aroused in speaker and listener. It is likely that the - d o r formations, like their Spanish equivalents, bestride the adjoining classes of nouns and adjectives, e.g., that they can be smoothly placed after the local expression for 'very.' On the other hand, there is no evidence that the corresponding feminines, whatever their function, are formed in -ora, on the model of, say, Sp. trabaj-ador-a 'working woman'; 'industrious' (f.) The chances are that Cabraniego, faithful to a deeply rooted pattern, contrasts (m.) - d o r with (f.) - d e r a;[66] one hint to this effect is b r e - a d - e r a, the name of a contraption used in baking

[66]On this point see my remarks in "Genetic Analysis of Word Formation," in Current Trends in Linguistics, ed. T. A. Sebeok, Vol. III: Theoretical Foundations (The Hague, 1966), esp. pp. 359-361—comments based in part on unpublished research by P. M. Lloyd.

bread (the dough is squeezed through its cylinders, a process known as
b r e - a r). The names of female workers and of engines have at all times
been equated in Romance.

Examples include c a c a r - e x - a d o r 'given to cackling, (fig.) to boasting, exaggerating'; l l e n d - a d o r 'guard in charge of the grazing cattle';
m u r - i - a d o r 'mason, wall-builder' (against the background of corresponding, self-explanatory verbs in - a r); l l i m - i d o r 'expert in knocking
fruit from a tree' (attached to l l i m - i r).[67]

214.3. Purely or predominantly nominal suffixes.

Such suffixes are fairly numerous and may be conveniently arranged on
the basis of a compromise between functional and semantic criteria:

(a) Adjectival abstracts (and mass-nouns). Here one finds such familiar
items as:

(α) - d á , whose link to the primitive may be a vowel or zero, esp. if
it has sunk to the level of a mere suffixoid: s e ñ a l - , s e ñ a r - d á 'pain-
ful recollection, nostalgia';

(β) - í a (sometimes expanded to - e r - í a): g o l - o s - í a 'sweet-
meat, delicacy, tidbit' (lit. 'eagerness, greediness'); also, with a less
neat cut between stem and suffix, b e l o r d - e r - í a 'excess, superfluity,
utterly worthless thing'; serving the need of sheer characterization in
p e x - i g u - e r - (í) a 'nuisance, calamity,' cf. coll. Sp. pejiguer-a, -ía
'worthless thing, troublesome thing' (Madrid). The accent is on conglom-
eration in f o l l - e r - í a 'large number of puddles,' 'path full of puddles,'
beside f o l l - e r u 'puddle,' which, in turn, flanks f o l l a 'soft clay';
z a b u y - e r - í a 'large amount of defective maize cobs,' beside z a b u y u ;

(γ) - (δ) - o r and - u r a , closely related in every respect and referring to comic, bizarre, censurable character traits or behavioral
features: b e y - u r a 'caprice, grimace, joke or jest' (note the stereotyped
phrase f a c é b e y - u r e s 'to make funny faces' and observe b e y - a r r -
a - e s [pl. of - a d a] 'tricks or doings of old folks'); b r a b - o r 'fierce-
ness, bravery' (cf. Sp. brav-eza, -ura); d e l i c a d - u r a 'morbid susceptibility'; f r i - u r a 'coldness'; t o c h - u r a 'madness, stupidity'; y a n - u r a
'oddity'; beside the primitives, semantically self-defined, b i e y u , (implied) b r a b u and d e l i c - a d a , f r í u , t o c h u , and y a n u . Of these

---

[67] Among other suffixes clearly astride the two form-classes one may mention
 - ó n , here examined at an earlier juncture (under the N-pillar), and - a n t e / - i e n t e ,
whose local representation happens to be conspicuously meager.

d e l i c a d - u r a marks a transition to the large class of deverbal - u r a
formations chiefly attached to the weak past participle, as in m a n c - a d -
u r a 'lesion,' beside m a n c - a r 'to hurt' (also refl.), s e r p i - , s i r p i - ,
x i r p i - a d - u r a 'liquid produced by an attack of herpes' esp. in a cow's
udder, beside s i e r p e 'herpes, (creeping) virus disease entailing the
formation of blisters on mucous membranes' (lit. 'snake')—presumably
via a verb s e r p - i - a r 'to w(r)iggle, slither,' cf. Sp. culebr-ear, serp-
(ent)-ear ; note the parallel triad r a s c - u ñ - u , - a r , - a d u r a , echoing Sp. rasg-uñ-ar 'to scratch.' An - u r a abstract ('bitterness') forms
the link between a m a r g u 'bitter' and a m a r g - u r - i e n t u 'embittered.'

Functionally related - a n z a / - a n c i a , as in s e g u r - a n z a / - a n c i a
'security,' has been assigned a pigeonhole among integrated suffixes.

(b) Verbal abstracts. Most of these have already been preempted by earlier discussions; thus, - a u beside - a d a (pl. - a e s) occupies a niche
under the D-pillar; unintegrated - (a) - u r a and its variants have, for economy's sake, been examined in conjunction with de-adjectival - o r / - u r a ;
this particular function of many-pronged - ó n has not been separated from
the others (see N-pillar); etc. However, two suffixes so far only incidentally
mentioned at this point deserve fuller treatment:

(α) - í u often suggests vibrations, back-and-forth movements, or
gyrations and may thus, in such cases, be labeled iterative; it may have
a broader, mass-noun meaning, esp. if the word occurs preeminently in
the plural; where making a noise is suggested, it closely matches the
Spanish "sound-suffix" -ido rather than -ío: c i m b l - í u 'vibration'
(alongside c i m b l - a r) ; d a r l o s a - b o q u - í - o s 'to die' (probably
a blend of a - f o g u - í - o s and b o c a 'mouth'; cf. Sp. a-hogu-ío 'con-
striction of the chest' beside a-hog-ar 'to smother, asphyxiate' and note
Sp. dar las boqueadas, boquear—image of fish suffocating out of water?);
a d o b - í - o s 'condiments for food' beside a d o b u 'fresh, unsalted pork'
and no doubt a verb paralleling Sp. adobar 'to dress, prepare, repair.'

(β) - m i e n t u is functionally closest to - d u r a , being separated
from it by a slightly less heavy emphasis on perfectivity (hence, on the
results of the action involved), a feature which endows it with a stronger
dosage of abstractness: a - f o r f u g - a - m i e n t u 'pressure, harassment'
(= - ó n) flanks a - f o r f u g - a r 'to drive, goad, harass' (cf. f o r f o g - ó n
'peak of any activity'); a - f o r o ñ - a - m i e n t u 'the rotting of wood, esp.
chestnut-wood' beside a - f o r o ñ - á - s e (- d u r a refers to the same
process, but also to its effect); a - g ü e y - a - m i e n t u 'casting of the
evil eye [a spell]' beside a - g ü e y - a r 'to cast the evil eye'; a l l o r i - a -

mientu 'amazement, bewilderment,' beside allori-ar 'to stun,'
mostly through sheer overwork; cf. W.-Ast. allouri-ar) and the post-
verbal alloriu; amori-a-mientu 'annoyance, molestation' beside
tar amor-i-au 'to feel dizzy,' amoriu 'confusion, dizziness.'
Where the effects (results, symptoms) of an action are more readily
observable than the action itself, -mientu is likely to be dispensed
with: afrell-ad-ura or -ón 'breach, breaking caused by a blow,'
beside afrell-ar. On the other hand, -mientu better fits human
moods and humors: a-son-sañ-a-mientu, a-tenr-ec-i-
mientu, a-trist-ay-a-mientu.

Quite marginal to the dialect's native system of verbal abstracts are the
few instances of learned (typically, ecclesiastic) -ción, veritable incrus-
tations, e.g., ament-a-cion-es (pl.) 'prayers for the deceased, recited
before mass, with full mention of each one's name.' At the opposite end of
the social and emotional spectrum, one finds the racy facetious use of
-iella attached to the past participle to suggest comical actions (short or
specific blows, suggested by -ada, -azu, and -ón); cf. a-garr-ad-
iella 'struggle, wrestling match' (reminiscent of Sp. agarrada 'quarrel'),
beside a-garr-ar 'to seize' (cf. Sp. pes-ad-illa 'nightmare' and the
countless jocular Portuguese words in -ad-ela); similarly a-purr-id-
iella and en-gard-id-iella 'fight, scramble,' en-torn-ad-iella
'upset, overturning,' a escond-id-iellas 'furtively' (cf. coll. Sp. a
escondidillas [D. Catalán]).

(c) Diminutives. Their grammatical vehicles form the hard core of
integrated suffixes (see supra, under C-, N-, and T-pillars); moreover,
within the various vocalic gamuts they are, typically, marked by the vowel i.
An exception, at first glance, was (m.) -iellu, (f.) -iella (= W.-Ast.
-ello, -ella), here analyzed under the rubric of the LL-pillar; actually, the
formations at issue no longer form any solid block. Speakers are busy re-
moving the obstacle posed by the atypicality of the -ie- diphthong (to the
extent that it is still represented within the ranks of diminutives) through
two mutually supporting maneuvers: (a) They gradually replace i e by i
(a process expedited by the lateral pressure of Castilian and other central
dialects), and (b) they slowly dilute the strictly diminutive or hypocoristic
ingredient contained in the suffix. After a palatal consonant -ie- may
yield to -e-; thus cuch-iellu and -ellu coexist for 'knife.' In other
contexts -ie- forms still prevail, in fact are allowed, in typically Asturian
fashion, to extend to pretonic syllables: ferb-iell-ar 'to feel a burning
sensation or fever (ferb-iella) in one's chest,' forn-iell-ar 'to
form piles of brushwood' (forn-iell-os); conversely, bain-ill-a

'green kidney bean' echoes Sp. vain-illa 'small pod, vanilla.'[68] The situation
is further complicated by occasional inroads of characteristically far-western
(Gal.-Ptg.) -elu, -ela, e.g., fard-ela 'kind of knapsack, a haversack'
(cf. fardo 'bale, bundle, burden,' a word far more common in Portuguese than
in Spanish), as against native far-iellu 'bran,' and mar-elu, -iellu
'yellow,' cf. Ptg. amar-elo vs. Sp. -illo. The semantic erosion of the suffix
(or of the homonymous suffixoid) appears in some of the preceding examples
as well as in cost-iella 'rib,' cuqu-iellu 'cuckoo,' mant-iella
'swaddling clothes,' mart-iellu 'hammer,' rest-iellu (or -iella)
'iron-pronged carding board.'

Among the unintegrated suffixes none proved to be less fit, in terms of
sound symbolism, for the role of a diminutive element than -uelu.[69] Its
final vowel, inopportunely enough, blocked any smooth interplay with -al,
-il (and the minimally developed -el, -ol), thus reducing the structural
value of its consonantal kernel, while the diphthong -ue-, singularly un-
welcome under the new set of circumstances, was phonically even farther
removed from the ideally suitable -i- than was -ie-. The result has been
the steady lexical decay of -uelu, -uela and, coincidentally, the rapid
loss of any unmistakably diminutive semantic substance (cf. the preceding
remarks on -iellu). Example: may-uelu 'clapper of a bell' beside
mayu 'wooden hammer'; the phrase da la parpay-uela 'to chatter,'
while for man-az-uela the reader is referred to men-az-uela,
which, tantalizingly enough, the author fails to list.

(d) Miscellaneous.

(α) -ambre, whose Spanish counterpart forms an attractive gamut
with either -imbre or -iembre and with -umbre (for one hint see Romance
Philology, XXI, 41), is exceedingly rare and structurally isolated in Cabraniego: a-llor-i-ambres (pl.) 'equipment used for yoking.' Since
the expected Asturo-Leonese form is -ame—witness fame 'hunger,' exame
'swarm,' -ambre is best explained as a case of sporadic borrowing
from a central dialect. The queer contamination with allori-ar 'to stun'

[68]From the stray vestiges of the reduction of ie to i let me select llangristu
'thin, lean'; 'roguish, mischievous, saucy,' a regionalism which seems to contain a
potent blend of 'narrow,' 'locust' (cf. llangosta 'bumblebee') and 'awn, beard of an
ear of corn' (ar-iesta > -ista), the whole secondarily contaminated by the
local word for 'tongue' (llengua; cf. llengu-at-eru 'garrulous, foul-mouthed,'
reminiscent of Sp. lengu-ar-az). For an example of ue > e see preba 'proof'
beside preb-ar 'to prove' (= Sp. prueba, prob-ar).

[69]On the roots of Sp. -uelo see J. R. Craddock's penetrating analysis in Romance
Philology, XIX (1965-66), 286-325, esp. 315-318, in criticism of F. González Ollé.

is also less astonishing if a lexical newcomer is involved. Cf. further (imported) e n s - a m b r - a r vs. (indigenous) e n s - a m - a r 'to swarm' (speaking of bees).

(β) - a n d r u : Because m e l - ó n and m e l - a n d r u are locally two rival designations of the 'badger' (elsewhere in the Peninsula this animal goes under such names as tej-o, -ón, -ugo), it seems permissible to posit a suffix - a n d r u, utterly unknown to Castilian. Its existence may have been one factor in the crystallization of f i l - a n d r - a d a 'miscellany of things strung on one thread,' though the expansion of the expected interfix - a n d - (cf. Sp. hil-and-ero 'spinner, spinning room'—see Section 211 [c], supra) to - a n d r - admittedly invites an alternative explanation; note OSp. adverbial -mient(r)e.

(γ) - e n g a : For this handful of nominalized adjectives geared to a suffix of Germanic provenience (quite weakly developed except in Cata-lan and in some adjoining varieties of Aragonese) it is difficult to detect a common denominator. B o l - e n g a 'neighbor's (or resident's) right to pick up fallen fruit from community property,' flanked by the phrase d i r a b o l - e n g u e or a b o l - e n g u e 'to engage in early-morning opera-tions to pick up fallen fruit,' recalls Sp. abol-engo 'ancestry, inheritance'; p e r e n d - e n g a 'earring, pendant' snugly matches Sp. perend-engue 'earring, trinket,' also jibes loosely with (coll.) perend-eca 'whore' and peren-g-ano 'so-and-so.'[70] As regards the fluctuation of the final vowel, contrast Sp. bland-engue 'soft, easy-going' (beside blando) with abad-engo 'abbatial, abbacy' (beside abad).

(δ) - i s m u , - i s m a —transparent Hellenisms in the historical per-spective—are, to the descriptivist, a pair of rare suffixes asserting them-selves mainly in the narrow fields of meteorology and physiology, from which they may strike out, by way of figurative meanings: c a l - i s m a 'sultry weather, hottest time of day' (beside two semantically close forma-tions exhibiting the c a l d - stem variant); p a r a x - i s m u 'exaggerated compliment, fuss(iness), pampering,' lit. 'paroxysm' = 'fit of acute pain, sudden violent action' (= W.-Ast. -ism-ada), and - i s m - e r u 'one given to ingratiating himself by showering such compliments.'

(ε) - a r d u : This suffix, almost unknown to Castilian (but cf. mosc-arda 'flesh fly, blowfly, blue-bottle,' -ard-ón 'botfly, hornet,' fig. 'bore'), more than adequately represented in Gallo-Romance alone, shows unsus-pected strength in Cabraniego, too: m o s c - a r d u 'board with a nail pro-

[70] One senses a pervasive, if loose, allusion to 'hanging (around), being suspended,' a hint presumably rooted in etymological conditions.

truding from its tip' (its pricking effect compared to the insect's sting?),
p a b - a r d u 'stupid' (like a turkey or a peacock?), p e s c - a r d u 'small
fresh-water fish.' (B i g - a r d - i - u 'wanton, licentious' = Sp. bigardo
stands apart in every respect.) Even more noteworthy is the use of this
element as an interfix. Spanish, it will be remembered, shows here the
free alternation of -ard- and -arr-, as in mosc-ard-/-arr-ón. Cabraniego
causes surprise by the exuberance of interfixal - a r d - and, still more
significantly, by the apophonic interchange of - a r d - and - u r d - in
this position alone, not word-finally. Hence l i b - a r d - o n a 'variety of
long-stemmed cherry'; l l a m p - a r d - / - u r d - i - a d a 'flare-up' (with
a pair of neatly matching verbs, in addition to l l a p - u r d - i - a r displaying a leaner stem); l l a m p - u r d - i - a z u (or - i - ó n) 'quick or
extensive flush'; l l a s p - a r d - e r u 'very lively, prattling and gossiping.'
Into this stock l l o m b - a r d - (i) a d a , - i - a z u 'noise from a loud fall,'
lit. 'cannon-shot,' easily wormed its way—receiving as it did secondary
support from l l o m b u = Sp. lomo 'back, crease, loin,' though actually
traceable to an amalgam of Lombardía (as the home of old firearms) and
bombard-e-ar; cf. Sp. lombarda 'lombard gun.'

214.4. Two verbal suffixes.

Of the two unintegrated verbal suffixes on record, - e c - e r and - i - a r ,
the former poses a few and the latter numerous and intricate problems, some
of them transcending the scope of this paper.

(a) The inchoative suffix - e c - e r may be attached to nominal, adjectival, and verbal stems—a division which yields a prime classification of its
constituents. A cross-classification is suggested by the coappearance of some
such prefix as a - , e n - , e s - , or else by its absence. A third attempt at
classification (here not further pursued)—along the semantico-syntactic axis
—might distinguish those formations which, true to their label, actually stress
inchoation (ingression, inception) from those which emphasize the graduality
of an entire transmutational process, quite apart from the group totally lacking in power of aspectual suggestion.

(α) Inchoatives extracted from nominal stems are few; cf. m a f -
e c - e r 'to become moldy, stale' beside m a f a 'sticky crust' (the matching adjective is m a f - i e n t u). One is left wondering whether a - t a p -
e c - e r 'to darken completely' should be attached to the local counterpart
of Sp. tapa 'lid' or of tapar 'to cover, obstruct (the view).'

(β) Inchoatives traceable to adjectives form the hard core of the entire
group. Whereas in Spanish proper they are ordinarily ushered in by em-,

en- if the primitive is short (en-loqu-ecer 'to madden,' en-negr-ec-er 'to blacken,' entorp-ec-er 'to benumb'), or by zero, if the primitive has a minimum of three syllables (humed-ec-er 'to moisten,' oscur-ec-er 'to dim, darken, becloud,' lobregu-ec-er 'to make or grow gloomy,' in rivalry with bermej-ear 'to turn bright red,' hermos-ear 'to embellish,' redond-ear 'to round off, out'), Cabraniego joins other varieties of Asturo-Leonese in favoring, in this particular context, a - over any other pre-fix, without entirely excluding e m - (e n -) or e s - : a - b e y - e c - e r 'to grow old' (= a - b i e y - á - s e , flanking b i e y u), a - c h o c h - e c - e r 'to become senile' (there is no separate mention of c h o c h u), a - g u a p - e c - e r 'to beautify' (= a - g u a p - a r , flanking g u a p u , inferrable from g u a p a - m e n t e 'to be sure, indeed, lots of'), a - l l o q u - e c - e r 'to drive crazy' (= - e n t - a r ; primitive omitted), a - m o y - e c - e r 'to moisten, wet, soak' (= - e n t - a r ; cf. m u e y u 'dripping, soaking'; the actual primitive is surely the equivalent of Sp. muelle 'soft'), a - p o d r - e c - e r 'to rot' (beside - e n t - a r ; associable with the locally well-represented adjectival p o d r - family), a - r r i q u - e c - e r 'to enrich' (r i c u may be taken for granted), a - s c u r - e c - e r 'to grow dark' (alongside e s c u r o), a - t e n r - e c - e r 'to soften up' (relatable to t i e n r u), a - t o c h - e c - e r 'to become foolish, silly' (t o c h u), a - t o s q u - e c - e r 'to coarsen, make uncouth' (the occurrence of t o s c u need not be doubted). The tendential polarization, familiar from Spanish, of the two competing parasynthetic frames a — a r   vs. e n - , e s - ---- e c e r (a-grand-ar vs. en-grand-ec-er 'to enlarge'; a-clar-ar vs. es-clar-ec-er 'to clarify'; exceptions: em-bot-ar 'to dull,' en-tibi-ar 'to make lukewarm') is, consequently, alien to Cabraniego. One finds sporadic vestiges of the less favored patterns: e m - p r o b - e c - e r 'to become impoverished' (perhaps for the sake of sharper contrast to etymo-logically unrelated p r o b - e c - e r 'to swell, increase in volume, soak in water [e.g., wheat]')[71] and e n - (as a variation upon a - devoid of any special significance) g u a p - e c - e r , see supra. E s - , locally preferred to d e s - , does yeoman's service in e s - c a l - e c - e r 'to heat up, warm up'; (refl.) 'to become heated' beside e s - c a l - e n t - ó n 'heating' (the primitive is basically adjectival; for the prefix cf. Fr. é-chau-ff-er, OSp.

---

[71] I would take as a starting point PRŌDESSE, not in its classical sense of 'being useful to, benefiting someone else,' but in the plausible derivative sense of 'profiting from, drawing benefit, thriving,' cf. Sp. pro 'advantage,' obs. prov-encia (documented in UCPL, I:4, 126), and provecho 'gain, profit' < PRŌFECTU 'advance, headway, success.' It is difficult to understand how p r o b - e c - e r and e m - p r o b - e c - e r , being semantically at loggerheads, can coexist at all.

es-cal-ent-ar[72]); es-fr-ec-er 'to get cold or cooler' (beside friura, etc.; the truncation of the stem, reminiscent of the loss of the e-
in a-scur-ec-er, may have been expedited by the semantic conti-
guity of frescu); es-mor-ec-é-se 'to become livid and numb,
from an excess of choking tears.'[73]

(γ) Inchoatives traceable to verbal stems (of the type represented by
Sp. es-trem-ec-er 'to shiver') are either sparse or show few departures
from the standard language. Al-borr-ec-er 'to hate,' the counterpart of Sp. aborr-ec-er and of Engl. abhor, shows the expected change
in segmentation resulting in the infiltration of the pseudo-Arabic article.
An unhealable split has occurred between pa-ic-er 'to seem, appear'
(which involves the unusual, post-vocalic allomorph -ic-er) and
apr-ec-er 'to make one's appearance, climb to a vantage point in
search of something.'

(b) The Asturian suffix -i-ar functions basically like Sp. -e-ar, as in
guerr-e-ar 'to wage war' (cf. Fr. guerr-oy-er) viewed in its relation to
guerra 'war.' It also corresponds to Sp. -iar, whose i ingredient represents
no accretion vis-à-vis the nominal primitive (rabi-a 'fury' ~ rabi-ar 'to
rage,' limpi-o 'clean' ~ limpi-ar 'to cleanse'). This foreseeable conflation
of the two etymologically and functionally disparate suffixes has occurred
in other branches of Hispano-Romance as well, entailing peculiar consequences, notably in Portuguese;[74] characteristic of Asturo-Leonese is the
widespread contamination of the primitive itself by the /j/ element which
has jelled in the verb, with the concomitant reduction in status of the

---

[72]For once -ec-er and -ent-ar are not freely interchangeable within the
frame of this word family; witness a-call-ent-ar 'to caress, treat a sulking
person with affection in order to dissipate his resentment' (involving the change
*lie > lle as in OSp. lievo 'I carry' > mod. llevo).

[73]The author associates this picturesquely defined verb with Sp. mor-ado, lit.
'mulberry-colored'; perhaps she has in mind a-mor-at-ado 'turned purple, made
black and blue.' Conceivably the dialect speakers do indulge such fanciful associa-
tions. In the historical perspective, at any rate, OSp. and OPtg. es-mor-ec-er is
merely an outgrowth of MOR-Ī 'to die'; see my article "Español morir, portugués
morrer, con un examen de esmirriado, morriña, murria y modorra," Bulletin
hispanique, LVII (1955), 84-128.

[74]Of the -i-ar verbs, most (abreviar 'to abridge,' anunciar 'to announce,' apreciar
'to assess, appreciate,' variar 'to vary,' etc.) stress the i in rhizotonic forms (abrevío
'I abridge,' as against Sp. abrévio); some, through confusion with the -ear verbs, substitute ei for i, thus: agenceio ~ -ciar 'to solicit, canvass, be an agent for,' negoceio
~ -ciar 'to negotiate,' premeio ~ -miar 'to reward, give an award to,' remedeio ~
-diar 'to remedy, palliate, amend,' on the model of nomeio ~ -mear 'to name,'
passeio ~ -ssear 'to take a walk.'

-i-ar morpheme. To exemplify the point: The word for 'wall' must originally have been *muru, from which, secondarily, mur-i-ar 'to build
walls' and, tertiarily, muri-a-dor 'wall builder' branched off. But once
the primitive has been allowed to adopt, through contamination with the verb
and with the latter's satellite, the lengthened form muriu, it is no longer
admissible, at least not for the descriptivist, to invoke the derivational -iar
suffix in stating the relationship of muriu to muriar; synchronically,
the two words display the same scheme of interdependence as do Sp. limpi-o
vs. limpi-ar (and no longer that of guerr-a vs. guerr-e-ar). Consequently,
the initial, readily predictable increase in the ranks of -iar, through convergence of two near-homophones, has, in the end, been more than balanced
by an unexpected loss through reshuffling of all elements entering into a
hierarchy.

Within the small residue of authentically generative -i-ar verbs one
may distinguish between (α) straight derivation, and (β) parasynthetic derivation, involving one of the common, semantically empty prefixes:

(α) got-i-ar 'to drip' (beside implied gota 'drop'), mozqu-i-ar
'to cut out a chip from an edible chestnut's hard shell before roasting it'
(beside muesca, dim. mozqu-ete, -eta 'nick, notch, chip, small
chunk'[75]);

(β) a-prad-i-ar 'to rake together into one heap the [mowed?] grass
scattered throughout a meadow,' fig. 'to take possession of things belonging
to another' (presumably alongside prau); not only the radical -d -
but, interestingly, the original suffixal -e - , generally blurred through
synalepha, has been neatly preserved in tertiary derivatives: a-prad-

---

[75]The major difficulty for the diachronist lies in this: In default of adequate records,
one can appeal only to plausibility in arguing that the coinage of mur-i-ar in fact
preceded the intrusion of /j/ into muriu. The reverse sequence of events is also
—though perhaps not equally—conceivable. Or take Sp. grad-a 'harrow,' -ar 'to harrow,'
as against Cabr. gradia and gradiar, respectively (W.-Ast. grad-ar faithfully
reflects the tradition, cf. GRADUS 'step, tier'). One considers the /j/ insert as representing a fairly recent innovation, be it only because the maintenance of the D is
here best understood on the assumption that it was flanked on both sides by A's at the
critical evolutionary stage (cf. the analysis of the D-pillar, above); but the decision
as to whether grad-ar was first expanded to -iar and grada followed suit, or whether,
conversely, the movement actually started with the elaboration on the noun, engulfing
the verb in the end, almost dwindles to a matter of the analyst's personal taste, given
the objective state of indeterminacy. Cf. the article ("Five Sources . . . ") mentioned
in the Prefatory Note.

e - o s 'remnants of grass left in the meadow after the raking,' p r a d - e - a
'extra-large tool used in this raking operation.'[76]

214.5. Adverbial suffixes.

Apart from putting to use, in molding its adverb, a few hypercharacter-
izing final augments (such as - a or - s), either separately or combined
(a s i n - a 'thus'; a n - a n t e - s, - a n t i - a, - a n t(r)i - e s, with obligatory a > e before - s), the dialect permits adverbial derivation only
along a single and familiar track: through attachment of - m e n t e to the
feminine form of the adjectival qualifier. In the process, the word may
acquire an unexpected meaning; thus b i z a r r a - and g u a p a - m e n t e are
both tantamount to 'lots, a good deal,' and the latter, if pronounced with an
appropriate melodic curve, also stands for 'sure!' (= Sp. ¡Ya lo creo! ¡Es
cierto!).[77]

[76]Lack of space forces me to leave out of reckoning the intricate network of derivational relations involved in the coinage of all secondary - a r, - e r, and - i r verbs,
which ideally should have been examined with full attention to the interplay of conjugation class and prefix. Thus, even limiting our scope to the none too numerous - a r
verbs ushered in by e m - , e n - , we could generate sentences showing that the primitive is embedded as a subject or as a direct object in the matrix of the verb; in the
latter case, the exact relation may, in turn, be one of affectivity (to put to use sth.
already existing) or one of effectivity (to produce sth. before it can be applied to any
purpose). Other possibilities (reference to time, locale, instrument, etc.) can be
easily superadded. Cf. b o r r - í n (a) 'fog' beside e m - b o r r - i n - á - s e 'to appear,
sweep in' (speaking of fog); e m - b a n - i e l l - a r 'to use as props hazel rods split
length-wise' (b a n - i e l l a, b a ñ - e l l a); e m - b a r - a r 'to build a fence from sticks
or poles' (b a r a, which also means 'lever, beam, rudder'); e m - b o t - i e l l - a r 'to
stuff (with food), satiate' (b o t - i e l l u 'animal's stomach'); e n - g u e d e y - a r 'to
trap, ensnare, leave caught or suspended' (g u e d e y u 'tangled device used for en-
trapping'), etc. The complete analysis of the overabundant material would require a
monograph-length investigation. In this domain, incidentally, rudimentary procedures
of generative grammar were used by Romanists more than half a century ago.

[77]The preceding survey of derivational suffixes does not aim at exhaustiveness,
least of all as regards loosely floating pieces of driftwood. Thus, while - a b l e and
- i b l e, so luxuriant in other Hispano-Latin dialects, are here conspicuously absent
from the ranks of fully developed morphemes, an occasional derivative may always,
in an unguarded moment, have slipped past the most self-contained speech community's
barriers, hence e r m a n - i b l e - m e n t e 'in brotherly, compatible fashion' (cf. Sp.
herman-able). The suffix of Sp. hall-azgo '(reward for a) find' lacks any adequate
representation in our inventory, but one discovers two pieces of lexical bric-à-brac:
unattached a y - a l g a 'hidden treasure' (alongside a - f a y - a r 'to find') and m a y o r -
a z u 'primogeniture'; cf. Section 211 (q). I have given no serious consideration to the
possibility of an autonomous CH /č/ pillar, because the author's relevant field-notes

are far from unequivocal on this score: She lists, on the one hand, the nouns f o r g -
a x a , - (u) i x a beside - (u) i t a 'shaving (of wood)'; on the other, among corresponding verbs, not only e s - f o r g - a x - a r and - (u) i t - a r , but also, inexplicably,
- a c h - a r and - (u) i c h - a r , all four defined 'to shave wood.' Again, she equates a
completely isolated d e s - f i l - a c h - a r with Sp. <u>deshilar</u> 'to unravel, fray'; Spanish
presents, harmoniously poised, both <u>hil</u>-<u>acha</u> 'shred, raveling' and <u>des</u>-<u>hil</u>-<u>ach</u>-<u>ar</u>
'to pull ravels (from a fabric),' and it may well be that this latter Spanish word has
found its way into Cabraniego.

PART THREE

CONCLUSION

310. Summary.

Though our survey of Cabraniego affixes was principally geared to the task of experimenting with a new alignment of categories: integrated vs. unintegrated, we fortunately made several other, incidental discoveries of varying scope and weight. It turned out, for instance, that the chosen sub-dialect of Asturo-Leonese is singularly poor in certain suffixes elsewhere copiously represented, e.g., among adjectives, -able and -ible (speakers use -ad-eru, -id-eru instead) and, among nouns, "Western" -ame and -ume (or, for that matter, -ambre and -umbre, to cite them in somewhat more "central" shape). Fairly meager, too, was the share of -engu (so generously displayed by Aragonese, as -engo and under the guise of -enco), and there was no evidence of any such -angu, -ingu, -ongu, or -ungu forms as might have allowed us to build a separate vocalic gamut around -NG-, as is admissible in many varieties of Hispano-Romance, on both sides of the Atlantic.

The paucity of abstract suffixes (as against, say, mass-nouns) was clearly perceptible throughout; particularly spotty was the representation of adjectival abstracts, with -era and -ura[78] somewhat more frequently in evidence than were -dá and -ez(a), virtually unidentifiable. Verbal abstracts, whether postverbal action-nouns or standard derivatives in -mientu and -ad-ura, -id-ura, appeared in fairly large numbers, a circumstance probably connected with their well-known propensity toward concretization ('action' → 'result, place of action').

The consequences of phonetic erosion for the vitality of suffixes were observable at several points. One was reminded of the effects of dilapidation where one contrasts the vigorous structure of the Latin triad -$\bar{A}$G$\bar{O}$, -$\bar{I}$G$\bar{O}$, -$\bar{U}$G$\bar{O}$ with its pitiful remnants in the dialect: -én, -ín (endangered by its diminutive homonym, of different provenience), and -uña. Particularly

---

[78] If it were possible to segregate the use of -era for sicknesses and physical defects from the tangle of its remaining functions, one might defensibly group this nuance of -era with -ura as one additional instance of an extra-short vocalic gamut.

dramatic was the local disarray of a whole cluster of suffixes generally supported by Hisp.-Rom. -d- [ð] traceable to Lat. -T-. In Cabraniego, this
consonant has survived in just a few contexts, e.g., f. sg. -a d a , but pl.
-a e s and m. sg. -a u ; -u d u as against -e u (Sp. -udo, -edo) and -i u
(this latter, as a result, matches both Sp. -ido and -ío).

Learned suffixes and suffixoids were not altogether absent, but they were
few and far between (cf. -e n c i a) ; moreover, the shape or the meaning of
the words in question showed all manner of bizarre distortions, misappre-
hensions, or adjustments to parochial needs. To round out our earlier supply of examples, m o n d - , m u n d - i c i a stands for 'dirt, filth' (in lieu of
etymologically correct inmundicia, as used in Spanish). Lausberg has judi-
ciously remarked that it is not even certain to what extent n a c i ó n 'new-
born domestic animal,' p a c i ó n 'green grass growing in the meadow or
freshly mown,' p r i s i ó n 'chain used to attach calves to the manger' can
be ranked as "cultismos," especially in view of the coexistence of t o r -
c i ó n and -z ó n 'colic'; analogously, if a z ó n 'brood or litter of lice'
reflects (N)ĀTIŌNE, it might be paired off with n a c i ó n (the other etyma
here at issue are PĀSTIŌNE, PRAEHĒNSIŌNE, and TORTIŌNE). One could
similarly analyze ñ i c i u 'seed readied for sowing' < (I)NITIU as a borderline case between learned and vernacular transmission.

Interdialectal borrowing was seen at work on an astonishing scale, since
not a few radicals appear in Galician-Portuguese disguise, as is demonstrably
true of those lacking an expected -l - or -n - between vowels. It there-
fore caused no special wonderment to discover a few deposits of -e l u ,
traceable to the Atlantic coast, beside a solid mass of examples of indigenous
-i e l l u and a few specimens of Castilian-inspired -i l l u . More important
than this detail was the coexistence of a whole vocalic gamut in two shapes,
native -a y u , -e y u , -i y u , etc. and patently imported -a x a , -e x u ,
-i x u , and the like, a bifurcation which repeated itself in the realm of verbs.

One novelty of the approach here essayed consisted in the systematic
rather than desultory confrontation of genuine suffixes, suffixoids, and interfixes. The second and third of these categories have, of course, long been
known under a profusion of names; but the standard procedure, after proper
identification, has been, by and large, to eliminate them from further discussion in characterizing and inventorying authentic derivational suffixes. In
the present study, the three classes were kept apart as tidily as possible,
but their interlocking (in the static perspective) and their steady interaction
(in the dynamic perspective) have at no time been disregarded. On account
of the typical structure of a Hispano-Romance derivational suffix—it begins
in perhaps nine out of ten cases with a stressed vowel—the true suffix, which
can be separated from a readily identifiable primitive, and the mere suffixoid,

which is welded to no neatly contoured radical endowed with a meaning of
its own, are tied together by a rhyme, i.e., by an exact phonic coincidence
ordinarily paralleled and reinforced by a hazy grammatical resemblance
(as when the words at issue, aside from the homophony of their final segment, also pertain to the same form class). This link by means of a rhyme
rather than through straight morphological division represents an interfer-
ence with the simpler derivational processes; to be specific, an intrusion
of phonology. The advantage of analyzing interfixes as an autonomous class
of morphemes—a treatment to which there exist weak alternatives—has long
since been expounded, and the issue need not be pressed again. As interfixes
are, by definition, pretonic in Romance, they are barred from acting as
carriers of the rhyme and thus offer a stronger appeal to the speakers'
sense of rhythm (syllabic count) than to their craving for an imaginative
phonic orchestration. Such vocalic gamuts as are observable in this category tend to be narrower and less richly motivated than corresponding
gamuts into which genuine suffixes tend to fall, but there are marginal exceptions to this general rule: Thus, accented -ardu alone was isolable
as a suffix, while atonic -ard- and -ord-/-urd- were arrayed in a
kind of staggered collocation. Moreover, one can establish a network of cor-
respondences between certain prefixes, on the one hand, and a substantial
number of suffixes and related elements, on the other; the semantically
empty prefixes almost entirely restricted to verbs, particularly a - and
em-(en-), enter into a variety of such interplays.

As regards the behavior of form classes, it has at all junctures proved
beneficial to separate verbs from substantives and, on one occasion, to sift
out from the mass of the latter still smaller classificatory units: formations
(a) preponderantly nominal, (b) predominantly adjectival, or (c) straddling
these two domains. The nominal sub-group invited a further division on the
basis of semantico-functional considerations: abstracts, mass-nouns, diminutives, etc.; only this much was salvaged of Meyer-Lübke's bold criterion for
restructuring, in mid-life (1921), the entire Romance derivational edifice.
The well-known relative weakness of the Romance verb, as compared to the
noun, in terms of derivational exuberance, was confirmed through the application of the new yardstick; particularly gratifying was the discovery that
every single vocalic gamut observable among verbs (e.g., those supported
by such pillars as -K-, -SK-, -X-) had its exact counterpart—as a rule,
more fully developed—among nouns; but the relation was not reversible.
Numerically, one witnessed the same trailing of verb behind noun in regard
to the unintegrated suffixes, but there were, for once, no one-to-one corres-
pondences, as with the gamuts.

The full measure of the dialect's current creativity and originality appeared in the ever-changing configuration of vocalic gamuts and in the ceaseless tentative introduction, literally before our eyes, of new consonant pillars,
especially -F-, -MP-, -Ñ-, and -P-. Whereas among unintegrated suffixes
the most noteworthy idiosyncrasies of Cabraniego were negative features
(varying phases of withering, total absences, and the like), we detected
among the integrated suffixes a record of steady ebullience and proliferation.
The grid that we have established through the use of vocalic gamuts and consonantal pillars as our two prime axes enabled us to recognize, at a glance,
certain gaps or empty boxes (slots), strikingly reminiscent of the Prague
phonologists' "cases vides"—lacunas dramatized as late as the mid-'fifties
by spokesmen for that school of thought; every such vacancy hides a "latent
suffix" and carries with it, as it were, an invitation to speakers, if not an
outright imperative, to fill it promptly. Not only are we thus privileged to
witness vigorous current attempts at paradigmatic expansion, but we can
almost predict future directions of such growth, provided of course—this is
the real crux—that the dialect's vitality remains unimpaired and the slant
of its mechanism stays unchanged. One inevitable by-product of the development of this network is the increasingly sharp symbolic characterization of
each stressed suffixal vowel. Whereas in Latin diminutives the role of the
vowel was negligible to the point of justifying, upon occasion, its total omis-
sion (VET-ŬL-US, from VETUS, beside PUEL-LA, from PUER), the identification of í with diminutiveness has become so intense and compelling in
Cabraniego as to have opened the door for the infiltration of Castilian -illo
alongside autochthonous -iellu (soon in preference to it?) and to have pre-
cluded the further spread of -uelu, after semantically eroding its residue.
Admittedly, this spectrum of phenomena is of an evolutionary nature, but
since, on indirect evidence, the processes in question are still continuing
unabated, in fact, presumably with increasing momentum, they cannot with
impunity be excluded from any balanced description. At this point Cabraniego
offers a superb example of the partial overlap of synchronism and dia-
chronism.

320. Genetic analysis.

Some of these considerations and conclusions can be translated into the
language of distinctly genetic analysis or, at least, demand clearly statable,
closely circumscribed inquiries before such a transfer from one perspective
to another can be safely carried out. Canellada cogently argues that Cabraniego at one time belonged to the Eastern variety of Asturian, an alliance
of rural dialects from which it has been gradually divorced (though the

recession of h u e - before f u e - [ɸwe] need not point to an earlier shift
F > h). A systematic inquiry into the lexicon of the neighboring Villaviciosa
dialect to the East, as codified by B. Vigón, and subsequent comparison, with
Cabraniego material, of its suffixal distillate, should allow us to set off, in
the domain of derivational morphemes, the presumably original stock of the
chosen East-central dialect, to identify its ties—through kinship and infiltration—to the loosening bundle of the Peninsula's Northwestern speech forms,
and to pinpoint any and all subsequent deflections due to the new pressures
exerted by racy Oviedo parlance and by the nearest "central" (i.e., Castilian-
ized) dialects, if not by Castilian proper.

330. Obscure suffixes.

Far more rewarding in methodological insights is the application of the
"suffixal grid" to the study of the so-called obscure suffixes of Hispano-
Romance, those refusing to fall into any clearly silhouetted pattern of Latin-
medieval-modern relationships. The temptation to trace them to a prehis-
toric, substratal tongue is indeed very great, and not all such identifications
thus far proposed need be brushed aside in cavalier fashion. Nor is there
much point in limiting one's search for sources to these archaic deposits,
especially in view of the continued vitality of the processes at issue. A separate ever-present starting-point for new suffixes is the false segmentation
of words—particularly of outlandish items borrowed from other languages
and dialects[79]—as well as the incessant disintegration of the older stock of
compounds, with which all Romance dialects, averse to composition except
along certain tracks, play reckless games.[80] It is not difficult for speakers
to extract a quasi-suffixal $\underline{F}$ or $\underline{P}$ from lengthy words so mutilated, then to
pad or bolster $\underline{P}$ by expanding it to $\underline{MP}$. The further success of these playful
experiments may very well hinge on conditions of internal economy presid-
ing over the dialect's total resources: If, for instance, the dialect has, from
time immemorial, one string of $\underline{C}$ /k/ suffixes and another string of $\underline{T}$ suf-

[79]On the enhanced susceptibility of borrowings to fluctuation see the classic pro-
nouncement of J. Gilliéron and M. Roques, "Mirages phonétiques," in their Études de
géographie linguistique d'après l'Atlas Linguistique de la France (Paris, 1912), pp.
49-80.

[80]A good example of disintegration of compounds is f r a n g ü e s u 'large bird of
prey,' which in the last analysis involves OSSIFRAGU 'sea-eagle, osprey' (with its
two constituents reversed). I do not include among compounds such binomials as
involve either reduplication or minimal variation, used in nursery words (c u r r i,
c u r r i 'run!'), animal calls (g ü i s a, g ü i s a [to frighten hogs], g u ó . . . g u ó
[to bring a herd of cattle to a stop]), and jocular coinages (c é n g o l e m é n g o l e
'ill-fitting or ill-suited dress'—somehow related to the 1st p. pres. ind. of ceñir 'to
reduce' and menguar 'to narrow').

fixes (both already overburdened with functions and filled almost to capacity
with vocalic variations), then the temptation for speakers to exploit the practically untapped potentialities of, say, a parallel P-string—given the inherent
affinity of /p/, /t/, and /k/—is almost irresistible. Another illustration of
the same principle: Assuming - a s c - can be effortlessly traced to a pre-
historic language, there is scarcely any need for our going to any great
length in searching for a comparably archaic source of, say, - i s c - and
- u s c -, so long as we agree to credit our dialect and its congeners with
prolonged potency in matters of apophonic variation. Placed within the grid,
- a s c - (or, for that matter, - a r r -) was likely to generate, under its own
power, an appropriately rich vocalic gamut. Thus any unduly strict separa-
tion of substratum research from structural analysis becomes, in the end,
indefensible.

INDEX OF CABRANIEGO MATERIAL

INDEX OF CABRANIEGO MATERIAL

(Compiled by Margaret Sinclair Breslin)

The references are to sections and/or footnotes.

anant(r)ies 214.5

andecha n. 12

antoxadiegu 211 (d)

antoxar 211 (d)

apalpar 121; 122; n. 3; n. 49

apalpayar 122

apalpuñar 122; 123; n. 49

apañucar 115

ap(i)egaízu 115

ap(i)egadiegu 115; 211 (d)

ap(i)egadura 115

ap(i)egar 115

apodrecer 214.4 (a)

apodrentar 214.4 (a)

apradeos 214.4 (b)

apradiar 214.4 (b)

aprecer 214.4 (a)

aprobetayau 115

apurridiella 214.3 (b)

arbeyal 211 (e)

arbeyu 211 (e)

argaña 211 (i)

ari(e)sta n. 68

arra(m)puñar n. 49

arrascuñar n. 49

arriquecer 214.4 (a)

ascurecer 214.4 (a)

asina 214.5

asombríu₁ n. 36

asombríu₂ n. 36

asonsañador n. 32

asonsañamientu 214.3 (b)

asonsañón 211 (g)

asonsañar n. 32

atapecer 214.4 (a)

atechá-se 121

atenrecer 122; 214.4 (a)

atenrecimientu 214.3 (b)

atochecer 122; 214.4 (a)

atopadiegu 211 (d)

atopaízu 211 (q)

atopá-se 211 (q)

atosquecer 122; 214.4 (a)

atristayamientu 210; 214.3 (b)

atristayar 122

atristayá-se 122

ayalga n. 77

azapatau 122

azurdiellar 121

azón 310

babá-se 212 (d)

babaya 212 (d)

babayada 212 (d)

babayar 212 (d)

babayosu 212 (d)

babayu 212 (d)

bainilla 214.3 (c)

balagar 112; 114; 211 (g)

balagarín 211 (g)

balagarón 211 (g)

baniellu n. 76

bañella n. 76

bara n. 76

begada 112

belordería 214.3 (a); n. 33

bentán(u) 133; n. 5

berañu 211 (i)

berde 211 (d)

berdiagazu 211 (q)

berdiagu 211 (q)

berdiasca 211 (l)

berdiascazu 211 (q)

berdona 115

berdugu 211 (d)

berduzona 115

bergüétanu 114

bericiu 112; 114

beriénzanu 112; 114

beriya 113

foruñu   211 (i); 214.1

frangüesu   n. 80

frescu   214.4 (a)

fríu   214.3 (a)

friura   214.3 (a); 214.4 (a)

fuelle   211 (a)

fueu   211 (n)

furaca   211 (a)

furacu   211 (a)

furaquera   211 (a)

furar   211 (a)

furaxaca   211 (a)

furruñosu   214.1; n. 40

furruñu   214.1

fusa   133

fusau   133; n. 36

fusu   133; n. 36

gafu   212 (f); n. 16

garduña   211 (q)

garitu   115; 211 (n); 212 (f)

garrar   212 (f)

gastizu   211 (q)

gatuña   211 (q)

gatuñazu   211 (q)

gatuñón   211 (g)

gayada   211 (c)

gayasperu   211 (m)

gayola   211 (m)

gayón   211 (c), (g)

gobeta   211 (n)

gobetu   211 (n)

gochacu   211 (a)

gochazu   211 (q)

gochu   211 (a), (q)

godobiellu   211 (f), (p)

godoyu   211 (f), (p)

golfarada   211 (c)

goliatu   n. 58

golifar   n. 55

golor   211 (e); n. 51; n. 55; n. 58

golosía   214.3 (a)

gorfilones   211 (g)

gorgolitu   211 (n)

gorgutar   211 (n)

gorguyos   211 (p)

gorollu   211 (f)

gorupa   n. 55

gorrumba   211 (g); n. 55

gotiar   214.4 (b)

goxa, -u   214.2

goxeru   214.2

gradia   n. 75

gradiar   n. 75

greñu   211 (i)

guañar   211 (i)

guañu   211 (i)

guapamente   210; 214.4 (a); 214.5

guar(i)ar   211 (a)

guarica   211 (a)

güe   211 (g)

guedeyera   214.2

guedeyosu   214.1

guedeyu   214.1; 214.2; n. 76

güeyada   121; 211 (c)

güeyu   121; 211 (c), (d); n. 16

guindón   211 (g)

güiña   211 (i)

güiñar   211 (i)

güisa güisa   n. 80

gui(y)ada   211 (c)

guña   211 (i)

guó guó   n. 80

gurgutar   211 (n)

gurria   n. 55

gurriapu   n. 55

gurrión   n. 55

gurrumba   211 (g); n. 55

gurrumbín   211 (g); n. 55

gurrumbu   211 (g); n. 55

macete   211 (n)

madera   211 (e), (i)

madreña   211 (e), (i); 214.2

madreñada   211 (c)

madreñar   121

madreñeru   214.2

madreñes   121; 211 (g)

madreñón   211 (g)

mafa 214.1; 214.4 (a)

mafecer   122; 214.1; 214.4 (a)

mafientu   214.1; 214.4 (a)

magostar   110

magüestu   110

magüetu   114

magustar   110

mana   211 (g)

manazuela   214.3 (c)

mancadura   214.3 (a); n. 32

mancar   214.3 (a); n. 32

mancorniar   123

mancorniazu   211 (q)

mancurniu   211 (q)

mancuspiu   123

maniega   211 (d)

maniegu   211 (d); n. 37

manina (de Dios)   211 (g)

mansolín   115

mante   211 (g); n. 3

mantega   211 (g); 214.2

mantegón   211 (g); 214.2

manteguera   214.2

mantiella   214.3 (c)

mantín   211 (g); n. 31

mantiquin   n. 3; n. 31

manu   211 (d)

marelu   214.3 (c)

mariellu   214.3 (c)

Mariña   211 (g), (i)

mariñán   211 (g)

martiellu   214.3 (c)

maseira   214.2

masuñar   110; 123; 211 (g); 212 (f)

masuñón   211 (g)

masuñu   110

matoxu   211 (o)

maurecer   122

maurientu   214.1

maya   133; 211 (a)

mayar   121

mayorazu   211 (q); n. 77

mayu   121; 133; 214.3 (c)

mayuca   211 (a)

mayuelón   n. 31

mayuelu   214.3 (c); n. 31

mazacuada   211 (c); n. 54

mazacuar   211 (c); n. 47

mazada   211 (c)

mazcayón   211 (g)

mazcayu   211 (g)

mazorga   214.2

mazorgueru   214.2

mear   211 (g)

mederizu   115; 211 (q)

melandru   211 (g); 214.3 (d)

melerizu   115; 211 (q)

melón   211 (g); 214.3 (d)

memerizu   115; 211 (q)

méngole (céngole . . .)   n. 80

meña   211 (a)

meñaca   211 (a)

meón   211 (g)

merenducar   212 (a)

merucu   211 (a)

mesar   211 (j)

mesoriar   121

mesories   121; 211 (j)

meta(d)a   211 (c)

metrinariu   211 (j)

mexacán   123

podrigañu   115; 211 (q)

podrizu   115; 211 (q)

polboreu   n. 60

pollascu   211 (l)

poner   121

poquerriñín   115

poquiñín   115

porconzón   115

pradea   214.4 (b)

preba   n. 68

prebar   n. 68

prisión   310

probe   115

probecer   214.4 (a); n. 71

probetayu   115

probiquín   n. 31

rabadal   115

rabadiella   115

rabal   115

rabexina   115

rabexíu   115

rabexón   115

rabexura   115

rabia   115

raigañu, -ón   n. 13

ramalazu   211 (q)

ra(m)puñar   n. 49

rapazacu   211 (a)

rapazu   211 (a)

rascadura   214.3 (a)

rascuñar   214.3 (a); n. 49

rascuñu   214.3 (a)

recostín   115; 122

recostinar   115; 122

recosti(y)á-se   122

redeña   211 (i); (m)

rellambé-se   121

rellugada   121

remocicar   121

remolinar   121

repostiegar   112

repostiegu   112

resalibau   121

rescocer   121

resgatu   211 (n)

resgón   211 (g), (n)

resqu(i)ebra   121

restiella, -u   112; 133; 214.3 (c)

restiellar   112

retafila   121

retay-a, -u   121

retorcigañar   115; 121

retrucar   121

riestr-a, -u   n. 16

riñir   212 (b)

riñuscar   212 (b)

robexíu   115

roblatu   211 (n)

roza   131

rozada   131

rozar   131

rozu   131

ruñentu   211 (i)

ruñosu   211 (i)

ruñu   211 (i)

sabadiegu   114

sábadu   114

sábana, -u   114

sacagüeyos   123

saltadera   115

saltapraos   115; 123

saltaricu   115

saltona   115

sallar   n. 42

sallón   n. 42

sallu   n. 42

sanixuela   211 (o)

sarapullo   n. 42

xirpiadura   214.3 (a)
xuan   123

yanu   214.3 (a)
yanura   214.3 (a)

zabuyería   214.3 (a)
zabuyu   214.3 (a)
zurdiell-a, -u   121